In praise of God's goodness, may you be happy

My Life's Song
In the Key of G

Gayle Goetten Piché

©2017 by Gayle Goetten Piché
All rights reserved. This book or any portion thereof
may not be reproduced or used in any manner whatsoever
without the express written permission of the author.

ISBN 978-1-938911-42-2

Cover Layout: Gayle Goetten Piché and Bridget Lea Halloran
Graphic Design: Terri Peterson
Jacket Photography: Dianne Goetten Krause
To contact the Author or for orders:
Email address: gj@gjpiche.com

Printed in the U.S.A. by
Smith Printing, LLC, Ramsey, MN 55303
(800) 416-9099 • www.smithprinting.net

DEDICATED TO MY PRECIOUS MOTHER
WHO INTRODUCED MUSIC AND SUNSHINE
INTO MY WORLD...
AND TAUGHT ME, BY EXAMPLE,
THAT JESUS LOVES US ALL THE SAME
(SEE YOU AGAIN IN HEAVEN SOME DAY)
AND TO MY FAMILY,
THE LOVES OF MY LIFE ON THIS EARTH!
YOU ARE, "MY LIFE'S SONG!"
I LOVE YOU FOREVER, "G" XO

Preface...

May you find just a little encouragement in a word,
in a thought, in reading my poems, my sentiments,
my silly songs. This world is demanding indeed!
Every day we are challenged to the max,
at times it seems, stretched beyond ourselves.
The Author, Leo Tolstoy, once said that "the purpose of poetry is to
provoke feeling in the reader, to "infect" the reader to induce
a change of conscience that may lead to a change in the world."

Instead of the "ice-bucket" challenge, I now present you with a different kind
of challenge. I challenge you to be "all of whom God created you to be"...to share that
love inside you with the world around you... to embrace your own song!
Let your own unique beauty shine! Let's challenge one another to "LOVE."
This world needs it now as never before!
To accept, to SEE the other, to acquaint ourselves with each other and
ultimately to love one another with all of our differences.
We truly are One...
One race of human beings... One at heart...
let us go forth and be encouraged by one another to,
"Be Strong and Carry on with our own Life's Song!"

I end this with a word that I learned from my Friend and have come to embrace;
"Namaste"...an ancient greeting still used today... spoken with a slight bow
and hands pressed together, palms touching and fingers pointing upwards,
thumbs close to the chest. It represents the belief that there is a
Divine spark within each of us located in the heart, an acknowledgement
of the soul in one, by the soul of another. I bow to you,
I appreciate and see God, in you.
Namaste,

In Gratitude

IN THE JOURNEY OF CREATING THIS BOOK,
MY HEARTFELT THANKS GOES TO MY EDITOR AND
DAUGHTER, BRIDGET LEA, WITHOUT WHOSE TALENT,
SKILLS, TECH SUPPORT, ENCOURAGEMENT AND
CONSTANT PRODDING ALONG, THIS BOOK WOULD HAVE
NEVER BEEN COMPLETED!
I GREATLY APPRECIATE ALL YOUR ADVICE, HARD WORK,
PUTTING UP WITH MY QUESTIONS, RE-READING
AND PROOFING AND ENHANCING AND BEAUTIFYING
MY WORDS AND SQUEEZING IN THE TIME TO
DEDICATE TO MY DREAM.
OUR MANY, LONG HOURS AND DAYS OF WORKING
ALONGSIDE ONE ANOTHER…THRU LAUGHTER AND
TEARS…AND "HERE WE GO AGAIN," AND "WRITING
STORIES IN OUR HEADS," WERE MADE JOYFUL
BY YOUR UPBEAT SPIRIT. I LOVE YOU DEARLY!
YOU GLADLY GIVE AND FREELY SHARE
YOUR TIME AND TALENT, LOVE AND PRAYERS.
YOUR PATIENCE AND ENCOURAGEMENT…
ARE NOTHING SHORT OF "HEAVEN SENT."
REMINDING ME, I HAVE A MISSION…
BUT NOT FULFILLED BY ME JUST WISHIN'!
SO WORK, WE DID, AS MONTHS FLEW BY,
CREATING MEMORIES, YOU AND I…
SOME DAYS LAUGHTER…SOME DAYS TEARS,
PLENTY OF HOPE AND CHASED AWAY FEARS.
HILARIOUS TIMES! WHILE CAUGHT BY SURPRISE,
I SIPPED MY COFFEE…
OOPS, OUT IT FLIES!
"DON'T LOOK AT ME WHEN I'M NOT READY,"
I SURE CAN'T HOLD MY COFFEE CUP STEADY!

• • •

SO, ON WE GO AND YES, YOU GUESSED...
MY DAUGHTER AND I WERE INCREASINGLY BLESSED...
WITH TIME, WITH LIFE, WITH PRECIOUS DAYS,
TO WRITE MY BOOK AND GIVE GOD PRAISE.
THANK YOU, MY DAUGHTER, WITH ALL MY HEART!
AND SO MY BOOK I NOW IMPART...

MAY MY READERS BE BLESSED OR MAYBE SMILE
OR JUST RELAX AND READ AWHILE...
MY LOVE TO ALL WHO MIGHT BE TOUCHED
AND MAY GOD BLESS YOU, OH, SO MUCH!
REMEMBER, BE STRONG AND CARRY ON...
WITH YOUR OWN LIFE'S SONG!
LOVE,

"Just Mom & Me" ♥

In Gratitude

To each one of my "cheerleaders," whether near or far away...my Husband and encourager, who gave me the space, love and support to spend many hours, days, weeks in my "writing zone." To my Daughters, both beside me and in Texas "rah, rah," over the phone and by text, my Siblings, Grandchildren, In-Laws and Friends, I thank you for your support and encouragement to go forward.
Your kind words fill my heart!
My heartfelt thanks to my Sister and Friend, Dianne Karen, for her artistic advice and talent and her generosity in the use of her beautiful, original oil paintings, which she allowed me to share in this work!
My Grandson, Jack, who has contributed his original drawings...
And all who have allowed me to use their photos.
I am thankful for every day I've been given, for "Every day is a gift, that's why we call it the present."
I am thankful that the song of my life has continued for this long...
my every step growing closer to the finish line.
May we seek His Kingdom together;
From a heavenly place,
Beyond time and space...
May God bless my words to fill you
with His grace,
May His precious love be shown to you
and His care revealed in all you do.
To God be the glory!

"J"

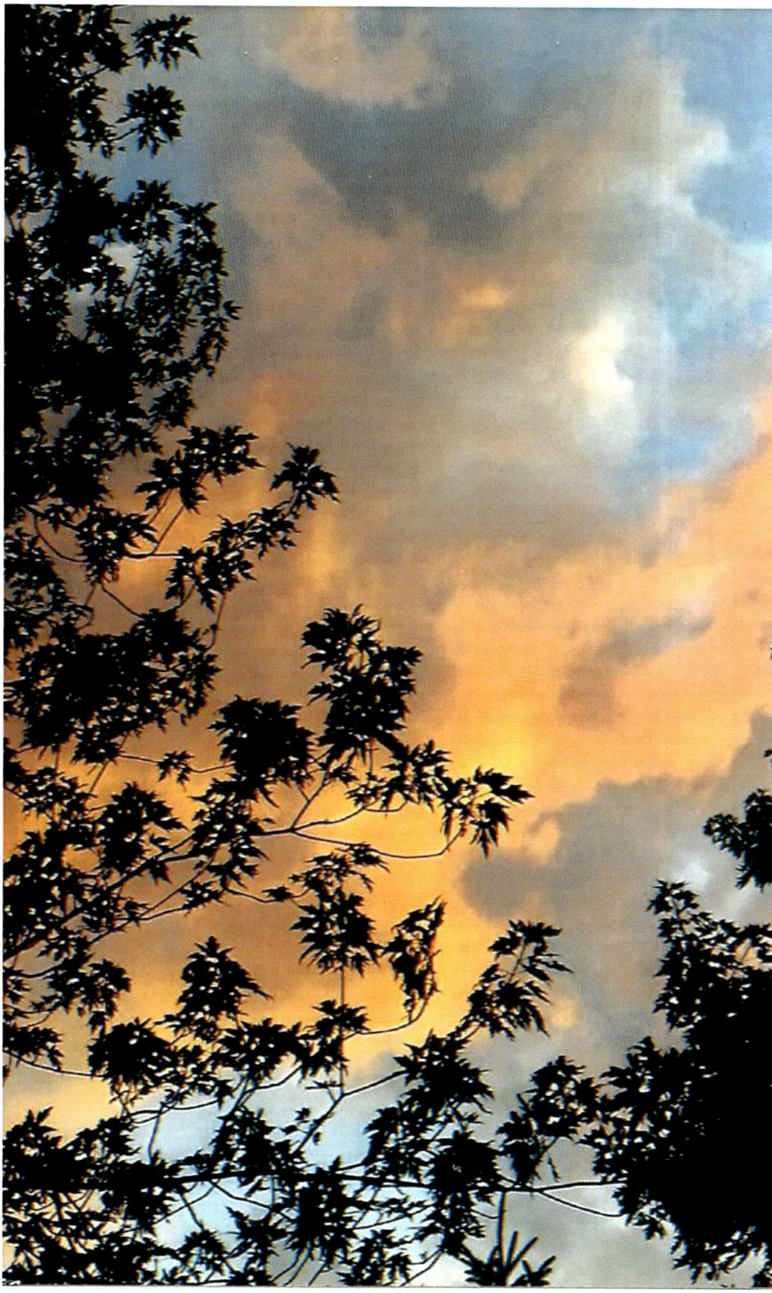

Table of Contents

MY LIFE'S SONG IN THE KEY OF "G" 1

Chapter 1:
INSPIRATIONS ON THE DIVINE 2, 3

Mountain of Life 4, 5
God Lives In Each of Us 6
Decisions 7
His Touch 8
His Kingdom On Earth 9
In The Silence Of The Morning 10, 11
This Is All I Need 12
A Quiet Reminder 13
Heartbeat 14
God's Spirit Is Alive And Well 15
I'll Never Be Hungry 16
God's Masterpiece 17
The Answer's There 18
Let The Carpenter Build 19
You Made This Heart Within Me 20
He Is All I Need 21
Be Still 22, 23
Because You Prayed 24
In Faith 25
Our Lives Are Rich In Meaning 26
Living For the Lord Who Loves To Lead You 27
Creator, God, is Very Near 28-29
Teach Me To Love 30
Great Love 31
Give Me Your Life 32
The Mystery Unfolds 33
My Heart Pours Out A Symphony 34
Sweet Faith 35

Chapter 2:
THOUGHTS ON ETERNAL LIFE 36, 37

The Eyes Of God 38, 39

We Never Walk Alone, Take His Hand 40, 41

Awake 42

The Beginning, Not The End 43

Our Loss Is Their Gain 44, 45

Chapter 3:
NATURE AND SEASONS 46, 47

Sleepy Dreams 48

Prepare To Be 49, 50

A Midnight Blessing 51

Heaven In A Moonbeam 52, 53

Moonlight Musings 54, 55

Summer Blessings Flutter By 56

Still Standing 57

A Springtime Morning Symphony 58, 59

April 60

A Golden 24 61

Journey To Earth 62, 63, 64

Countless Blessings 65

First Visit To My Ocean 66

Foamy Lace 67

Willow Weeping 68, 69, 70, 71

Chapter 4:
FAMILY 72, 73

Childhood Thoughts 74, 75, 76

Spreading Sunshine 77

She Gives Her All 78, 79

The 4Th Of July 2007 .... 80, 81

The 4Th Of July 2009 .... 82, 83, 84

Tears Over A Cheese Sandwich 85

Kisses 86, 87

My Heart Is Blessed 88

Sweet Blessings In Life, Siblings 89

A Little Valentine 90, 91

Snowflake 92

Snowbaby Sister 93

You Are You 94

Memories Unforeseen 95

Who Is That In The Mirror 96, 97

Through A Child's Eyes 98, 99

My Plea 100, 101

Encouragement From Beyond 102, 103

The Heart Of A Woman 104, 105, 106, 107, 108, 109

Chapter 5:
CHRISTMAS 110, 111

Tender Little Baby 112, 113

Christmas Is Here, Hosannas Ring 114

Keeping Christ In Christmas 115

The Greatest Gift Is Love 116, 117

Our Enchanted Christmas 118, 119, 120, 121

Happy Birthday, Jesus 122, 123

Who Or What Is Santa Claus? 124, 125

Chapter 6:
WHIMSICAL MOMENTS OF GRANDCHILDREN, FUN AND SONG 126, 127

I Wish, I Wish, I'd Catch A Fish 128

Sounds "Fishy" 129

I Won't Be Afraid 130, 131

I'm Only 4 132

Happy Jack 133

Let's Write A Poem, Gramma 134

My Wormy Wormy Story 135

The New Group	136, 137
Five Cents A Cup	138, 139
Popsicle Sticks	140
My Fishin' Song	141
Just Do It	142
A Wonderful Wednesday Adventure	143, 144, 145
A Wonderful Wednesday	146, 147
Little One	148, 149
Gabo, Bompa, Please Come See	150, 151
Treasures	152, 153
Soso	154
This Five Year Old Boy	155
Brother, Friend & Buddy	156
Behold The Child at Play	157
Today's Reality	158, 159
Here's Me.. Just Sayin'...	160, 161, 162, 163

Chapter 7:
FRIENDSHIP AND CARE FOR ONE ANOTHER 164, 165

Being Kind	166
Hearts That Listen	167
Just Stay Near	168
Pride	169
Refuges, Who Cares?	170, 171
Kindness Seeds	172
Can You See Me?	173
Remember	174, 175
Pass It On	176, 177
Butterflies And Broken Wings	178, 179

Chapter 8:
MEMORIES OF MOTHER AND AGING 180, 181

When I Grow Old	182
Mom's Poem	183
Age	184
Our Treasure	185

My Mama 186, 187
Memories While Shopping 188, 189
Our Dress Rehearsal 190, 191
The Eternal Song 192, 193
My Mother's Hands 194, 195
Absence 196
Hands 197
Without A Sound 198, 199
Peace In The Valley 200, 201
There is a Time for Every Purpose Under Heaven 202, 203

Chapter 9:
REFLECTIONS OF A CANCER SURVIVOR ... 204, 205
Dear Reader 206
Reflections Of A Cancer Survivor 207, 208, 209
As One 210
The Dance 211
Set Free 212, 213
Sweet Assurance 214
My Prayer 215
Press On 216, 217
Willow Whisperings 218, 219
The Master Of Design 220, 221
Waiting 222, 223
Picture This 224, 225

Heartfelt Tributes 226-233
Heartfelt Thanks 234, 235

My Life's Song
In the Key of "G"

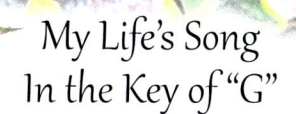

All of us have our own "Life Song." Our days are filled
with life's lessons. Opportunities to grow and to share
God's blessings with our fellow travelers along the way.
These writings are some of "My Life's Song."
I am a child of God, a Woman, a Daughter, a Wife, to a
Husband whose constant love and support I would never want to
do without, a Mother of two fabulous, grown Daughters,
kind and caring Sons-in-laws, Grandchildren, who are truly
"Grand," a Sister to six precious Siblings, a proud Auntie and
I have Friends who are real blessings in my life!
I have enjoyed being a Real Estate Agent for thirty years,
helping other's fulfill their dreams of owning their own home.
I am in the second half of my life now.
I have survived cancer twice, by the grace of God.
I have experienced a pathway of joy and sorrow, suffering
and healing, trials and victories, tears and laughter! I have learned
that in the eye of the darkest storms of my life,
in the very center of the storm, resides our loving God,
who is always there to meet us, to shelter, to guide, and to comfort us!
I open myself to you, my reader, and pray that you might be blessed,
if even in a small way and be encouraged to...
Be Strong and Carry on...
With your own Life's Song!

Gayle

Yet, in all these things, we are more than conquerors,
through him who loves us.
Romans 8:37

"Violin & Flowers"
Original oil painting by Dianne Goetten Krause

CHAPTER ONE
Inspirations on the Divine

Mountain of Life

We climb the mountain of life together,
Hand in hand and side by side...
Ever uplifting one another
With our Shepherd as our guide!

Through the mountains and the valleys...
Over rocky hills and trails;
Let us, together, sing His praises
As His peace and strength prevails!

Hold out your hand, oh my companion...
Whisper prayers, as on we trod
Closer, higher, leading upward...
To the mountain-top with God!

GOD, my Lord, is my strength;
he makes my feet swift as those of deer
and enables me to tread upon the heights.
Habakkuk 3:19

"Mountains"
Original oil painting by Dianne Goetten Krause

God Lives in Each of Us

I heard the voice of God today,
He called me on the phone…
And, through your voice, I heard Him say,
"You're loved and not alone!"

I felt God put His hand in mine;
A strong yet gentle touch…
When you placed your hand within my own
And said you loved me much!

I felt His warm encouragement
When you listened, as I talked…
And your eyes said, "Yes, I understand,"
"That path I've also walked!"

And, the letter that I just received
Hand-written, by a friend…
Surprised me…in the closing line…
God's signature was penned!

I am always with you;
You hold me by my right hand.
Psalm 73:23

*Flower design by
Jack Henry Nguyen*

Decisions

So many small decisions
They just piled-up inside...
And even just the tiny ones
Looked so huge, I could have cried!
'Twas then I felt the gentle nudge
That told me loud and clear...
"You don't have to make them all alone...
I don't want you to, My Dear!"
"Stop now and give them all to Me,
Set your racing mind at rest!
Use a little of that "stuff, called faith,"
Foolish Child, don't protest!"
So I wrapped up all the worries
Insecurities and fears...
And I placed them in a bundle
And I tied them up with tears...
And I lifted them above myself
Raised them to my Precious Lord,
And He reached for them, with loving hands
And my very spirit soared!
For I knew then, what He asked of me
Was to simply do my best!
When I used a little of my faith...
He took care of all the rest!

For this reason I say to you, do not be worried about your life, as to what you will eat or what you will drink; nor for your body, as to what you will put on. Is not life more than food, and the body more than clothing?
Matthew 6:25

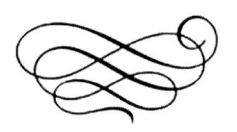

His Touch

You touched me...in my pain, I grew.
Your presence engulfed me
and I knew...
for how else could such pain be sweet?
And victory come, but not defeat...
You touched me, Savior,
With your hand,
Unworthy, though I feel I am!
You touched me.

*Then from behind Him came a woman, who had suffered
from a hemorrhage for 12 years, and she touched
the fringe of His cloak, for she said to herself, "if I can
only touch His cloak I shall be well again."
Jesus turned around and saw her, and He said to her,
"courage, my daughter, your faith has restored you to health."
And from that moment the woman was well again.
Matthew 9:20-22*

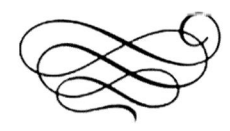

His Kingdom on Earth

We are His voice~~~
We are His hands~~~
We have a duty; we're privileged,
To do as He commands.

He sends a chance for us each day;
To show others He is there~~~
We are His voice and we should speak,
His gospel we must share!

He chose us for His people~~~
"Christian" is not just a name,
It's how we live and who's our Lord
And, what do we proclaim!

He put us here and gave us tongues,
His word "could" spread, like fire~~~
If we tried to love as Jesus did,
He'd be everyone's desire!

Let our hands give glory to Him,
Sweeten our speech with praise~~~
Let's share the "truth" with those we meet,
That it's Jesus who fills our days!

In the Silence of the Morning

In the silence of the morning,
When the dew is on the ground,
The presence of my Savior
Is apparent all around!
The chirping and the singing of the birds
That He has made,
And the happiness of their new day...
As they face it, unafraid.
They simply trust their Creator
For their food and for their bed;
While sweetly singing happily...
By His hand, they are fed!

*Are not five sparrows sold for two pennies?
Yet not one of them is forgotten by God. Indeed, the very hairs
of your head are all numbered. Don't be afraid;
you are worth more than many sparrows.
Luke 12:7*

This is All I Need

When my spirit sinks within me,
And my heart is in despair...
When I feel alone and frightened,
Oh, My Lord, you're always there!

Your word reaches in and touches me,
Into depths a friend can't go...
And Your healing presence strengthens me,
Oh, My Lord, I love you so!

When my dreams of life seem shattered,
And confusion settles in...
Your word speaks soft but clear, inside,
My Lord and I can win!

I won't try so hard to plan my life,
I will leave it to Your care...
And then, watch the blessings tumble down,
Oh, My Lord, You're always there!

The Lord is my strength.
Psalm 118:14

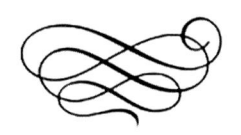

A Quiet Reminder

I planted a garden
pulled weeds, how I tried!
I was awfully upset,
When my garden died!

I laid out a day
With precision and care,
But my plans were all changed,
It just didn't seem fair!

I forgot, in my haste,
To first ask and see,
If that's what the Good Lord
Intended for me!

So, He gently stepped in,
To remind me today,
That things would go better
If I would just pray!

Heartbeat

God's love envelopes me;
He's as close as a whisper,
Or a tear,
Or a sniffle,
Or a blink of the eye!

His warmth encompasses my entire
being, and fills me to the brim.
His invisible love becomes visible
In others,
In situations,
In our family,
In our lives every day.

Our human heartbeat keeps time
With His time,
And the seconds
tick, tick, tick away.

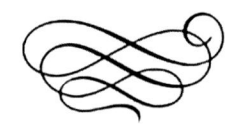

God's Spirit Is Alive and Well

Fellowship; a precious thing
To share with one another.
God's spirit is alive and well...
Thru a Sister and a Brother.

I can see Him moving in your life
And it strengthens all my days...
I can feel Him working thru your hands,
In your kind and gentle ways.

I can sense His warm love, way inside
And a peace that's deep and true...
For I see that God's alive and well,
And I see His love through you!

*Dear friends, let us love one another,
for love comes from God.
1 John 4:7*

I'll Never Be Hungry

You are the Bread of Life to me,
You're all that really counts...
And, only your hand holds the key,
As to what my life amounts!

I shall not worry for my future,
As to what life holds in store...
For tomorrow cannot bring me
Where "You" haven't been before!

And, as I love the children
You've entrusted to my care...
So, You're love for me's far greater,
It will follow everywhere!

You are the Bread of Life to me,
I shall follow where you lead...
So, light the path, that I should walk,
Your lamp is all I need!

Jesus said to them, "I am the bread of life;
whoever comes to me shall not hunger,
and whoever believes in me shall never thirst.
John 6:35

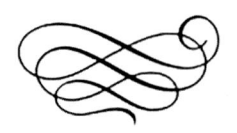

GOD'S MASTERPIECE

He keeps carving us and molding us
And when the pain gets great...
We want to say "Lord, stop a second,
Hold on... can't it wait?"

But He knows better far, than I
So the sculpturing goes on...
He's a Master of an Artist,
There'll be joy when pain is gone!

He knows just where to place the grooves
to complete His work of art...
And He has precision timing...
He knows when to stop or start!

We must trust this perfect Artist...
He's got the blueprint in His hand,
"So, carve away, yes, mold me, Lord
To a more perfect, loving man!"

The Answer's There

"You prayed that I would listen
So I'm calling, I am near…
You prayed that I would answer you,
So I'm speaking…can you hear?

If you listen, very carefully,
I'm trying so…to help you see,
If you'd just slow down your thoughts a bit
Then perhaps, you could hear me.

You needn't speak so loud…so long
For I am very near!
But My answers come most quietly,
I am speaking…do you hear?"

Let The Carpenter Build

The only way I can be fully alive
For the glory and honor of Jesus;
Is to empty myself, drain out all that I am,
For it's then, that the Lord's Spirit frees us.

He wants us to be more than we'll ever dream of,
More than we have the power to be...
We must die to ourselves to be vessels for Him
But we'll live for Eternity!

We must empty out all of our fears, deep within us
And tear down the broken, old walls...
Give Him some room to begin reconstruction
It's to "New Life" that our Jesus calls!

Better make way for a new and bright vision,
A new self... in the life of the Lord,
Then He'll fill us and free us,
That seems quite enough,
In just payment, for His room and board!

Therefore if anyone is in Christ, he is a new creation.
The old had passed away; behold, the new has come!
2 Corinthians 5:17

You Made This Heart Within Me

You made this heart within me,
May it throb with love for you;
You made these hands to serve your needs,
And, I'd best see they do!

You made these eyes, that fill with tears,
Gave me life; Yourself...
And you shower me with riches,
I'd best see I share that wealth!

You created my soul to love you,
You knew me before my birth;
So, I'd best seek Your plan for me...
All the days I'm here, on earth!

Before I formed you in the womb I knew you.
Jeremiah 1:5

He Is All I Need

Oh, the face of Jesus,
What a sweet thing to see...
To behold the face of my Savior,
My Rock, the One who sets me free!

Oh, to walk along life's pathway,
Together, my Savior and me...
Oh the sweet, blessed name of Jesus,
He is my everything, He is all I need!

– Bridget Lea Scott Halloran

Seek the Lord and His strength;
seek His face continually.
Psalm 105:4

Be Still

Let My peace envelop you
Let your restless spirit cease!
Be "still" and know that I am Lord,
So your faith, I can increase!

Quiet all your questioning...
I am speaking, child, be still...
Hear My voice and heed My call
Be conformed onto "My will!"

Be still...and know that I'm your Lord,
Your life's already in My hand...
And when you are shaped, as I see fit;
I will show you your life's plan!

Be still before the Lord.
Zechariah 2:13

Because "You" Prayed

Because you prayed for me today
God heard and answered prayer.
Because you prayed for me today
God displayed His loving care!
He heard your prayer and He reached down
And touched me, with His peace,
May our praise and thankfulness
For God's love never cease!!!

IN FAITH

Oh Lord, I give You my past,
My today,
My tomorrows,
They are Yours!

My past, for forgiveness…
My today, for faith…
My tomorrows, for strength…

For we know not what lies before us;
But rather, in faith,
Step on, ahead…
In Jesus name,
Unafraid and strengthened
By Your unyielding presence…
Amen, Lord, Amen

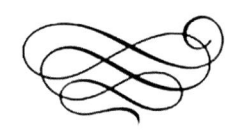

Our Lives Are Rich in Meaning

Our lives are rich in meaning
For each thing we do or say
Reveals oceans of significance,
In a sacred kind of way.
Only our Creator knows
The essence of a thought...
For the very depths, within our souls,
He fashioned, did He not?
He understands our inmost being
He knows every thought inside,
For He formed and called us, each, to life,
Our Creator will provide!
Our Father is protecting us
In the shadow of His hand...
And our day of birth or time of death,
Almighty God has planned.
His ever-constant, watchful love,
Is steadfast, pure and strong...
He knows the path and guides us home
As on the wings of dawn.

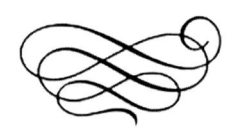

LIVING FOR THE LORD, WHO LOVES TO LEAD YOU

WHEREVER YOU MAY GO, WHATEVER YOU DO OR SAY...
GOD'S GREAT LOVE WILL BE WITH YOU IN EVERY WAY.
OH YES, HE HAS A PLAN;
LOVES YOU COMPLETELY...
THE LORD LOVES TO LEAD YOU,
KEEP HOLD OF HIS HAND.

FOCUS ON GOD'S WORD, FOCUS ON OUR LORD..
AND THE GREAT CELEBRATION
WE'LL ENJOY FOREVER MORE...
PRAY IN THE GREAT VICTORIES,
FOR THE LOST TO BE FOUND;
LET US RUN WITH ENDURANCE
WITH HIS PEACE, JOY, HOPE & LOVE!

An Encouragement Song
Written by Kandace Krause Goman

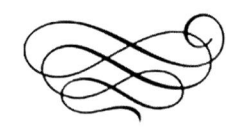

Creator, God, is Very Near

Sometimes if we're very still
And quiet in our heart...
We will feel God's presence very near
In our daily lives He plays His part.

He is so close, so real, so near...
Sometimes our eyes don't see
His love revealed in simple things...
His life...in you, in me.

In the newness of the springtime
His love beckons us to see,
That the power of His majesty
Is in every leaf and tree.

The miracle of His great love
Unfolds in every flower...
And the preciousness of life, itself
We are given, every hour!

We but have to gaze into the face
Of a loving, honest friend
To realize deep within ourselves
That Our lives will have no end.

If you watch a child run and laugh
With an aged one, say some prayers...
Or just listen to a bird that sings,
You'll believe in God, who cares.

• • •

He shouts to us in daily things
He pours out His love each minute
If we will but open up our hearts...
We will know God's presence in it.

Awake my soul! Oh hear, deaf ears,
My blinded eyes must see...
Creator, God, is very near;
He lives...in you...in me.

Praise the LORD! Praise the LORD, O my soul!
Psalm 146:1

Teach Me to Love

Gentle Father, teach this child,
Show me how to love;
Bless me with your guidance
And your wisdom from above.
Send me forth, to share Your love,
With others, day by day...
Allow Your light to shine thru me,
Show me, God, the way.
Grant me, Lord, a heart that cares,
A heart that's open wide...
Fill it with warmth
That it may beckon others,
Come inside.
Let me share a love that's strong,
In freedom, let it grow...
But then please hold me tightly, Lord
When it's time to let it go.

Great Love

Father, You have touched me,
I am warmed by Your great love
As tho a fire burns inside my heart...
With flames of praise to God, above.

For Father, just now You touched me,
I am filled with Your great peace...
I have felt the warmth of my Father's hand,
My cares wiped clean...A great release.

Your love has filled me to the brim
And healed me with the touch...
The daily tensions melt away,
For You love me, very much!
For I have felt my Father's touch,
His kind and gentle way...

And I am warm with a peaceful love,
For He touched my heart, today!

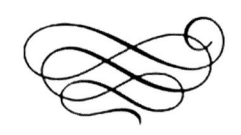

Give Me Your Life

GIVE ME YOUR LIFE...I'LL TEND IT WITH CARE

SING ME YOUR PRAISES...BREATHE ME A PRAYER

DRAW ON MY STRENGTH...RELY ON MY LOVE

AND MY SPIRIT WILL FILL YOU

WITH PEACE FROM ABOVE.

The Mystery Unfolds

At the very core of our Christian faith
A mystery unfolds…
Not just the fact that Jesus died,
But the miracle is that He rose!
He felt pain, He suffered and died on a cross…
He was buried, without any glory,
He gave meaning and hope to all of our lives
Thru His Resurrection story!
Just as the buds burst forth in the spring…
And the flowers will bloom in the earth,
He's renewed and refreshed our souls with His hope,
He has given our lives a new worth!
We thank you, Lord Jesus, for being our hope
We will live on, forever, in You…
Now our death will not be a permanent thing
For our spirits will then be made new.
And for all that You've done and been for us
You seem only to ask one small thing…
That we love one another and that we believe
That You're Jesus, our Lord and our King!

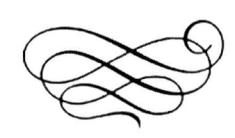

My Heart Pours Out A Symphony

My heart pours out a symphony
A symphony of praise...
To God, my Father, mighty King,
Who blesses all my days.

The music pierces thru my soul
I honor You, my King...
My heart beats now, in joyful strains
In praise of You, I sing!

Alleluia, You are good
And I am rich, indeed...
Praise and glory to my Lord,
Who gives me all I need!

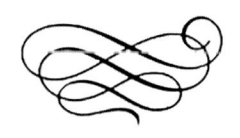

Sweet Faith

Faith is like the sweet notes
Trilling from the tree...
The bird, itself, I cannot see.

But sing, it will, and so close by
Carrying it's melody into the sky.

The morning song, sung joyfully
A true, rich blessing for you, for me!

This earth, this beauty, eyes to see...
Have been created for you, for me!

His sunshine slides across my face
This early morn I'm blessed with grace!

Soak in His warmth
Then, pass it on...
Your own life
Will become a song!

"Mother's Bible"
Original oil painting by Dianne Goetten Krause

CHAPTER TWO
Thoughts on Eternal Life

The Eyes of God

If we could have the eyes of God...
And look beneath the grass, the sod...
We would not find our loved ones there;
But in a place beyond compare!

If we see beyond our human grief...
Our painful hearts would sense relief,
For deep within us, we would know;
The peacefulness would come, would grow.

Our pain is sharp...and we must weep
For we know nothing of their sleep;
To rest, in Christ, must be divine...
We are the branches, He the vine.
His hands are gentle, arms are strong
To lead them home, where they belong.

Our loss so great, our ears can't hear,
The angel whisperings, "oh, so near."
Their silent kisses caress the air...
Their love, their memories everywhere!

Let us know joy, yet, while we weep
And grieve our loved ones, fast asleep,
Yet, tune our ears, our hearts to God
The soul is not confined to sod!
For we are given angel wings...
In endless sunsets, our hearts sings!

• • •

Our God has promised, He has said,
"your loved one sleeps and is not dead!"
Look up, have faith, wipe tears away,
We'll meet again, at home, someday!

*I am the Resurrection and the Life.
The one who believes in me will live
Even though they die.
John 11:25*

WE NEVER WALK ALONE…
TAKE HIS HAND

A FRIEND WILL HOLD YOUR LEFT HAND
AND OUR LORD WILL GRASP YOUR RIGHT…
THERE'S NO NEED FOR US TO GO ALONE
FROM THE "NOW UNTO ETERNAL LIGHT!"

FOR, OUR JESUS WENT BEFORE US
HE WILL GENTLY GUIDE US HOME;
AND HE'S PLACED THIS FRIEND, HERE, AT YOUR SIDE,
YOU SHALL NOT WALK ONE STEP, ALONE!

YOU BUT WALK INTO ANOTHER ROOM
THE DOOR IS OPEN, WIDE…
FOR, WE ONLY PASS FROM "LIFE TO LIFE,"
WITH JESUS, BY OUR SIDE!

Written when Grandma died January 11th, 1980

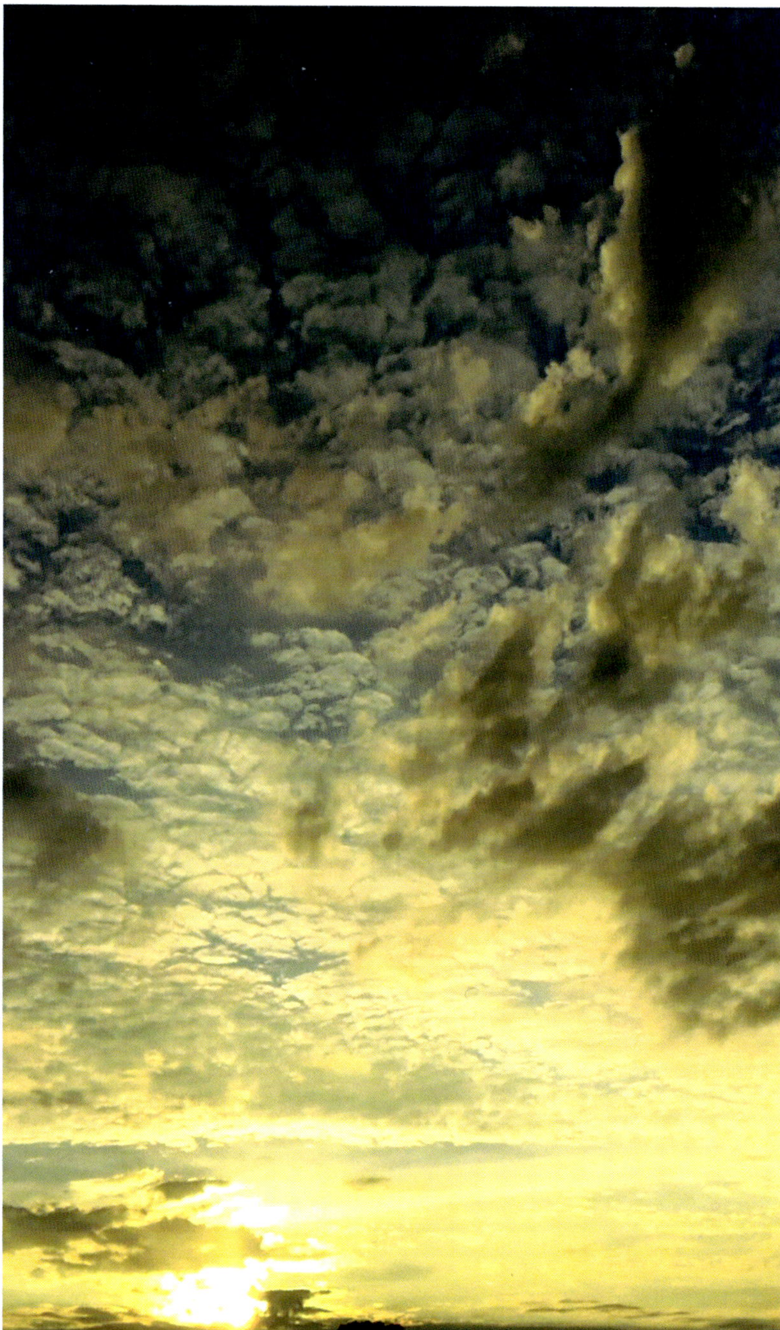

Awake

Awake, awake and put on strength
Sorrow and sighing will flee away...
The loneliness and pain are great;
But now awake to a brand-new day!

Do you not know?
Have you not heard?
Of the constant strength of God,
And that in His strength
Our wounds are healed...
We find comfort in His staff and rod!

Our weeping will endure tonight
But joy will come tomorrow...
For, in our faith, we trust His word
That joy will triumph over sorrow!

*Weeping may endure for a night,
but joy cometh in the morning.
Psalm 30:5*

The Beginning, Not the End

The warm breezes caress, as I sit on my swing
I've waited so long, now it's finally spring!
The sun's warm rays beating down on my skin
Make a person so grateful for this world that I'm in!

The crocuses are budding,
The trees are in bloom
And those daffodil's heads
will be peeking out soon.

What was once dead, in winter,
To be nevermore seen...
Are now peeking out
and the buds turning green!

It's a spring resurrection;
The dead comes alive
Through the warmth of the "Son"
We are made to survive.
So, rise up and shine
And give God your glory...
Because death...on this earth's
Not the end of our story!

OUR LOSS IS THEIR GAIN

LIFE GOES ON, NO MATTER WHAT ELSE HAPPENS TO YOU OR I,
THE SUN GOES DOWN, THE MOON WILL RISE,
AND PEOPLE WE LOVE WILL DIE.
AND LIFE GOES ON, AND STARS STILL SHINE…
EVEN IF EYES CAN'T SEE,
THE SNOW WILL MELT, THE GRASS WILL GROW…
THE FLOWERS WILL ALWAYS BE.
LIFE WILL GO ON, NO MATTER WHO IS CALLED BY GOD TO DIE
FOR WHAT WE CALL DEATH, THEY KNOW IS LIFE…
THEY SEE WITH A CLEARER EYE.
FOR WHAT BRINGS PAIN AND LOSS TO US
WHEN SOMEONE IS TAKEN AWAY…
BRINGS TO "OUR SOMEONE," JOY AND LIFE,
THAT WE'LL UNDERSTAND, SOMEDAY.
LIFE GOES ON FOR US AND THEM, A LIFE WE DON'T YET KNOW
BECAUSE OF THAT, WE HURT INSIDE,
BUT THEY'RE WITH GOD AND SO…
WE'LL TRUST THAT HE WILL CARE FOR THEM,
AT LEAST WE ALL MUST TRY…
TO TRUST OUR LOVING FATHER'S HAND,
TRUST, EVEN WHILE WE CRY.
FOR EVEN OUR LORD CRIED, WHEN HE LOST HIS FRIEND
AS HE RAISED HIM FROM HIS GRAVE,
PERHAPS TO SAY, IN A "HUMAN WAY,"
"TRUST ME, YOUR LIFE I'LL SAVE!"

• • •

SO, IF WE DON'T TRUST; HAVE HOPE IN GOD,
THERE'S NOTHING LEFT YOU SEE,
'CAUSE LIFE GOES ON; WHEN WE WISH IT WOULD NOT,
WHEN DEATH TOUCHES YOU OR ME.
THERE ARE REASONS BEYOND THAT "BEND IN THE ROAD,"
REASONS WE CANNOT SEE...
BUT HE'LL NEVER LEAVE US ALONE IN OUR GRIEF,
HE GIVES STRENGTH TO YOU AND TO ME.
SO, EVEN IF DEATH IS PAINFUL FOR US,
WHEN WE LOSE SOMEONE WE LOVE...
WE MUST THINK OF HOW JOYOUS IT MUST BE FOR THEM
TO BE WITH THEIR FATHER, ABOVE!
THERE MUST BE LIMITLESS HAPPINESS,
THEY MUST BE FILLED WITH PEACE...
SO, WE ASK YOU, LORD, GIVE US YOUR STRENGTH,
'TIL OUR PAIN AND LONELINESS CEASE.

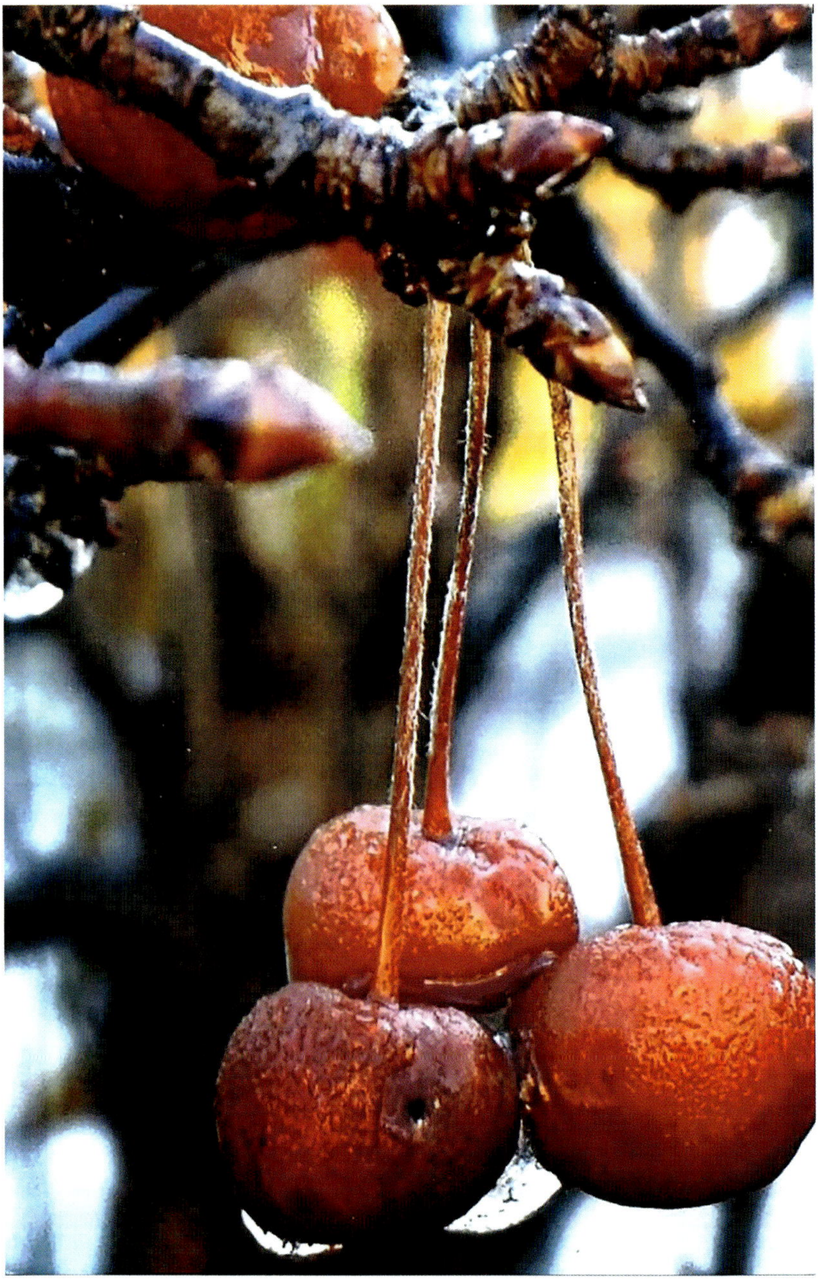

CHAPTER THREE
Nature & Seasons

Sleepy Dreams

Pastel colors,
        softly drifting...
Colors swirling,
        gently lifting...
Lifting spirits,
        twirling, swirling...
Violins and chimes abound,
        Colors swirling all around.
Hazy sleepy,
        soft and sweet...
Background drummers so discreet.
        Restful, Gentle,
            Peace filled song...
                Inviting you,
        to sing along.

Prepare to Be

I didn't expect the sun that day...
But it shined anyway.
I didn't expect the rain to stay...
But it poured anyway.
I wasn't prepared for life's ups and downs
And turn-arounds...
But they happened anyway.

One can't always be prepared...
Nor expect that you might be spared,
For life is full of unexpected happenings:
The thrills and joys and laughs and tears,
And endless fears,
They happen anyway!

So, the best that you can do...
is expect the unexpected!
And, as they say, "when the wind changes,
Adjust your sails," the way is then smoother...
Sail away with the wind to the unexpected Places...
and live!

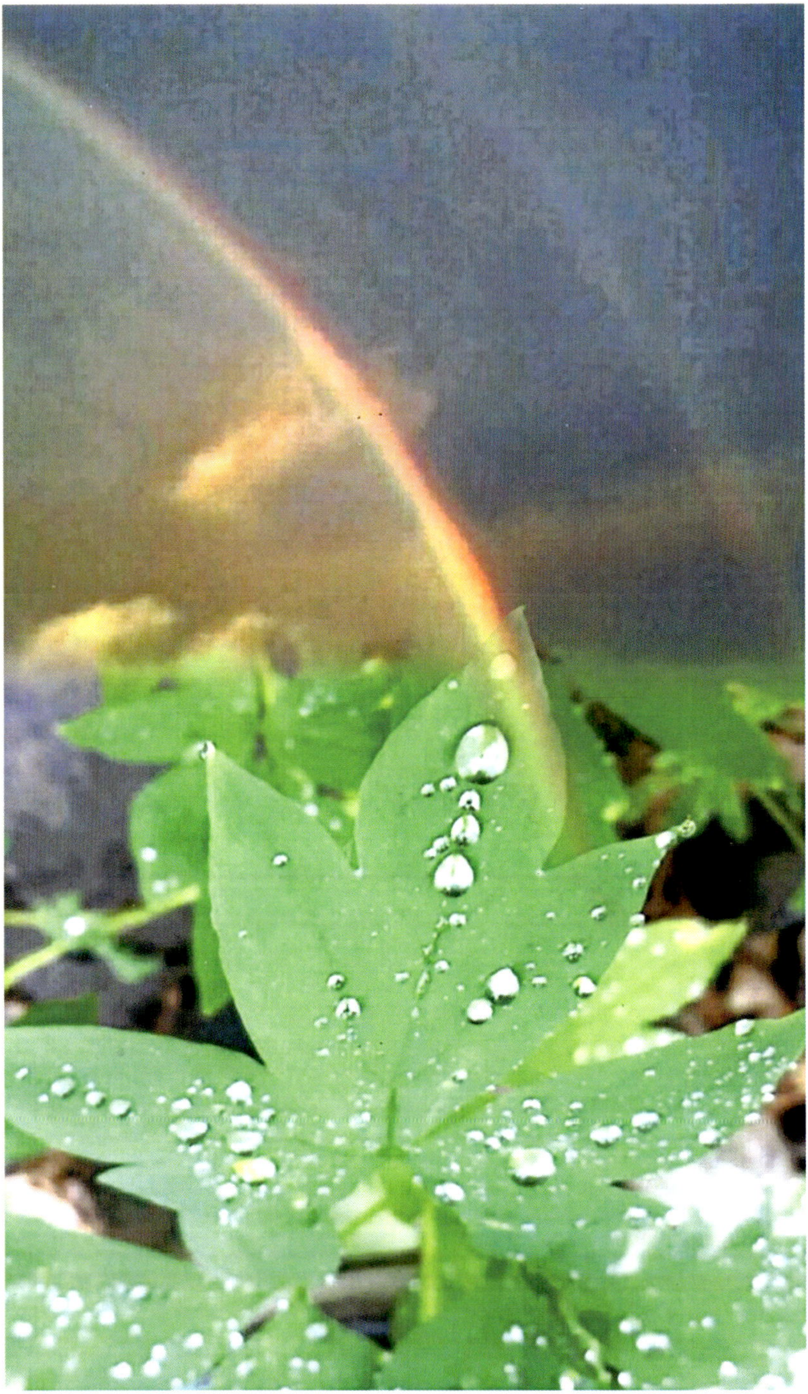

A Midnight Blessing

Silver strands of glistening rain,
Falling freely down the pane...
Dancing, dripping down the glass,
Diamonds sparkling in the grass.

Tiny droplets touch and slide,
As if enjoying their joyous ride.
A quiet, peaceful rain to hear...
As silent as a falling tear.

A sound so soft, it lulls your eyes,
And somehow holds them hypnotized.
To watch them sparkle radiantly,
Is soothing for the eyes to see.

And, now the sound is loud and clear,
A trickling to the ground you hear.
A cleansing, cooling rain tonight...
God's world washed clean
For a new day's light!

A dripping, drenching, rain-soaked earth,
The color green, a flower's birth...
A rainbow etched across the sky,
God's signature to you and I.

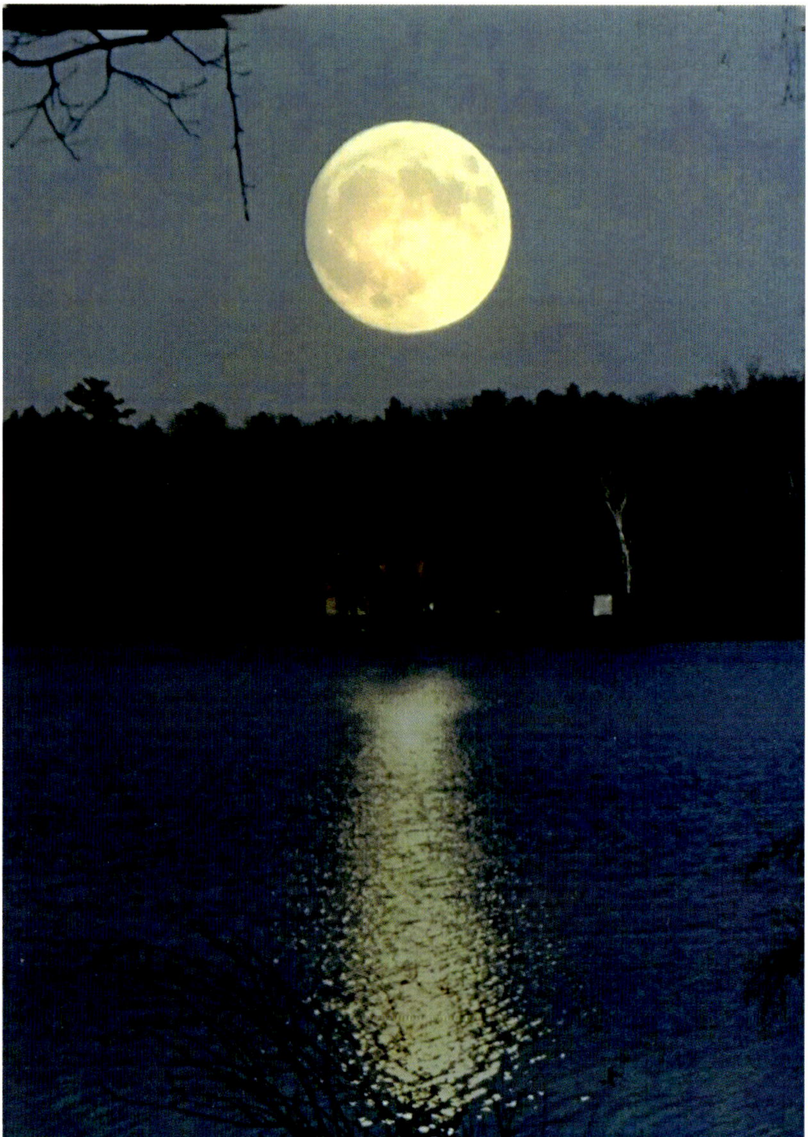

HEAVEN IN A MOONBEAM

A MOONBEAM SLID ACROSS MY PILLOW…
IT WOKE ME WITH A START;
SO I STEPPED INSIDE MY MOONBEAM,
AND WALKED TO IT'S VERY HEART.

ALL INSIDE WAS BRIGHT…IT SHONE!
IT WAS SOMEHOW DAY, YET NIGHT;
AND PEOPLE DWELT IN PEACEFULNESS,
IN ROBES OF GLITTERING WHITE.

THIS PEACE PREVAILED INSIDE MY MOONBEAM,
ALL WERE HAPPY AND SO KIND…
I GUESS THAT LITTLE MOONBEAM
WAS JUST "HEAVEN-ON-MY-MIND!"

How good and pleasant it is when God's people
Live together in unity.
Psalm 133:1

Moonlight Musings

Like a vapor rising high…
At dusk in the September sky~~~
Like an ember from the fire…
Rising only to expire~~~
Like the mist thats floating free…
Evaporates in the sun we see~~~
Like the trilling of a bird…
Who hides himself yet can be heard~~~
Like a feather on the ground…
That just appeared, no bird around~~~
A golden sliver of a moon, suspended in the sky...
Seems it almost winked at me~~~
as I go passing by…
As some petals on a flower~~~
Close up at night, they know the hour…
Like a raindrop, on your face~~~
That makes you giggle into space…
Like a hug that ignites a flame~~~
Inside your heart, you're not the same…
A gentle breeze brushes your face~~~
Somehow, that moment's filled with grace…
The sun that warms you, thru and thru~~~
Your body and your spirit too…
These fleeting pleasures do abound~~~
And, such are present all around…
One day our lives are here, then fly~~~
Taking our spirit into the sky…
And, as we pass, we leave a trace~~~
A heart we touch; kiss someone's face…

• • •

Or brush a hand; or blow a kiss~~~
But, we're still there, I'll tell you this!
Invisible to human eyes~~~
Our angel wings soar Into God's skies...
Yet, never leaving those we love~~~
Here in this life or life above...
I'm still the whisper in your ear~~~
I'm still the same, so do not fear...
I really never left you, Dear~~~
Hold out your hand, for I am near...
I'm closer than your whispered prayer~~~
My heart has heard, I will be there...
So, please embrace those tiny graces~~~
In all those unexpected places...
For only those who truly listen~~~
And are not too blind to see...
Will experience the miracle of life~~~
That truly sets us free.

~~~~~~~~~~~~~~~~~~~~~~~~~~

"Shhhh, be still, another miracle awaits you."

Written after a moon-lit boat ride on the lake,
Rippling waters and a sliver of a moon shining brightly above.

Summer Blessings Flutter By

The voices and the laughter ripple thru the summer air...
The chatter flies across the breeze...
as if without a care!
It echoes across the water...
'tis the days for lakeshore fun,
It's finally time to take a break
and bask beneath the sun!
How I love to sit and listen, to the voices, while at play,
Resounding from the other shore
on this cloudless, summer's day!
I hear another loud, "ker splash,"
and watch someone pull in a bass;
A toddler giggles, somewhere near,
"oooooooo, so cold," yet dives, no fear!
The breeze smells sweet...
like grass and flowers...
And I could sit for hours and hours;
While different birds trill out their song;
Inviting me to sing along!
I thank you, Lord, for days like these;
Your blessings flutter across the breeze,
Refreshing my heart, my mind, my soul,
I breathe my thanks, You make me whole!

Still Standing

I gazed upon the irises that in my garden grew,
The petals soft and velvety…
Softly rippled as they blew.
So delicate, so fragile,
I wondered as I watched…
How could they withstand the winds and storms
And somehow not be lost?
It was then that I remembered
The flower was from God…
Oh yes, a human hand had planted it in sod,
But somehow God takes care of them
And lets their beauty show…
To caress and bless our weary eyes
And perhaps to let us know…
That because of Him and all His care
For each of us every day,
We too, can weather wind and storms
Along life's rugged way.
We too, can stand up straight and tall
When burdens come our way…
For we know how and when to fall
upon our knees and pray.
We know our heavenly Father is watching and aware
Of every earthly happening
And every worldly care!

A Springtime Morning Symphony

I awaken to the golden sun rise that
illuminates the land, the water, the sky,
I awaken to a precious new gift,
"hand-wrapped" by my Creator, God.
All of Nature is alive and throbbing
with the heart-beat of springtime.
The evergreens danced in the wind and the fresh branches
twirled like flared, dancing skirts.
The clean, crisp colors of green,
of all shades, dazzled the landscape,
lush lawns turned emerald before my eyes.
Tulips opened and danced in the breezes of spring.
The ripples on the water seemed to laugh and lap loudly,
catching fish as they leapt in the air.
The rhododendron burst forth with purple flowers
and the rosy lights literally "turned on" with fuchsia color.
The lilacs adorned themselves in their
Sunday best frills and wore bonnets of lavender.
The sunshine shone warmly adding life to the waiting earth.
The trees, in unison, it seems,
glowed with a green tone at first...almost as if it were a mirage...

• • •

Then, suddenly, infant leaves uncurled...
Alive to springtime, a new birth.
The rains soaked and saturated the thirsty ground...
And the sweet smell of the spring, rain-soaked earth,
permeated the air.
The hungry robins hopped and listened
carefully for their supper of earthworms
promised to them by the plentiful rains.
The ruffly irises of lavender and yellow and deep purple flirted
with the breezes as the air gently caressed them.
The hostas' that surely seemed dead
underneath the weight of the winter's snow,
once again thrived and grew stronger and bigger than ever before.
The breath-taking sunsets bedazzled one's very being.
The promise of a new day's end and a hope
for tomorrow's new beginning.
This beauty of the Master's touch that ignited
and awakened the sleeping earth...
the Artist's brush strokes across the sky...
His loving touch upon the buds and flowers,
calling them forth to new life...
Calling us forth to everlasting beauty and sights
beyond our comprehension.
He speaks,
If we Listen...
We can hear...
We can feel...
We can touch the face of God this day!

APRIL

THE SUN-KISSED EARTH NOW COMES ALIVE...
WHILE BUDDING TREES BEGIN TO THRIVE,
THE BUSHES BOAST A GREENISH HUE;
GREEN PINES AGAINST A SKY SO BLUE!
THE CROCUS PEAKS OUT FROM BROWN EARTH,
ITS COLORS BLOOM FOR ALL IT'S WORTH.
A VIBRANT PURPLE, WHITE AND YELLOW
THE FIRST TO BLOOM, THAT EARLY FELLOW!
IT'S SPRING, THE EARTH IS BORN ANEW;
GOD'S SIGN OF HOPE FOR ME...FOR YOU...
TAKE TIME TO LISTEN, TIME TO SEE,
THE CHIRPING BIRDS, THE BUDDING TREE.
THE COLORS OF GREEN...THE SMELL OF SPRING
THE ROBINS ARE BACK AND ON THE WING.
THE TWEETS AND CHIRPS AND CHATTERING
THESE BIRDS ANNOUNCE RETURNING SPRING!

SLOW DOWN, TAKE TIME, WITH EARTH BE ONE;
APPRECIATE THE SETTING SUN!
AND, IN THE MORNING, AS YOU RISE...
GAZE DEEPLY INTO MORNING SKIES.
EMBRACE THE PROMISE, NOW AT HAND
AS GOLDEN RAYS AWAKE THE LAND
AND CREEP ACROSS THE FIELDS AND LAKE
'TILL EVERY BIT OF EARTH'S AWAKE!
ANOTHER SACRED DAY TO LIVE!
STRAIGHT FROM HIS HAND, OUR LORD DOES GIVE!

A Golden 24

We are all given the exact number of hours in any given day...
to use as we will use it. To live it as only we can live it.
24 golden hours, each and every day!
Will it make any difference that we were alive?
Will anyone's load be any lighter because of us?
Will anyone's heart be any brighter ...will anyone's pain be eased,
just a little, because of our caring hand, our own special touch, our individual smile?
Will we know, on this earth, that we have made a difference
or will we only become aware, in our eternal walk, that we have truly mattered?
We all know of a day or a time that someone's smile,
even that of a stranger, changed our day or maybe even our life,
but they never knew they made a difference.

So, we must continue to try to be supportive, to encourage, to smile,
to lift someone above themselves, above their pain, their worries.
We must continue to be God's servants, upon this old earth,
to serve, to lift, to pray for, others.
For it is our privilege, our duty, our responsibility, our mission,
Let us go forth...holding onto one another's hands...the clock is ticking...
24 golden hours await...

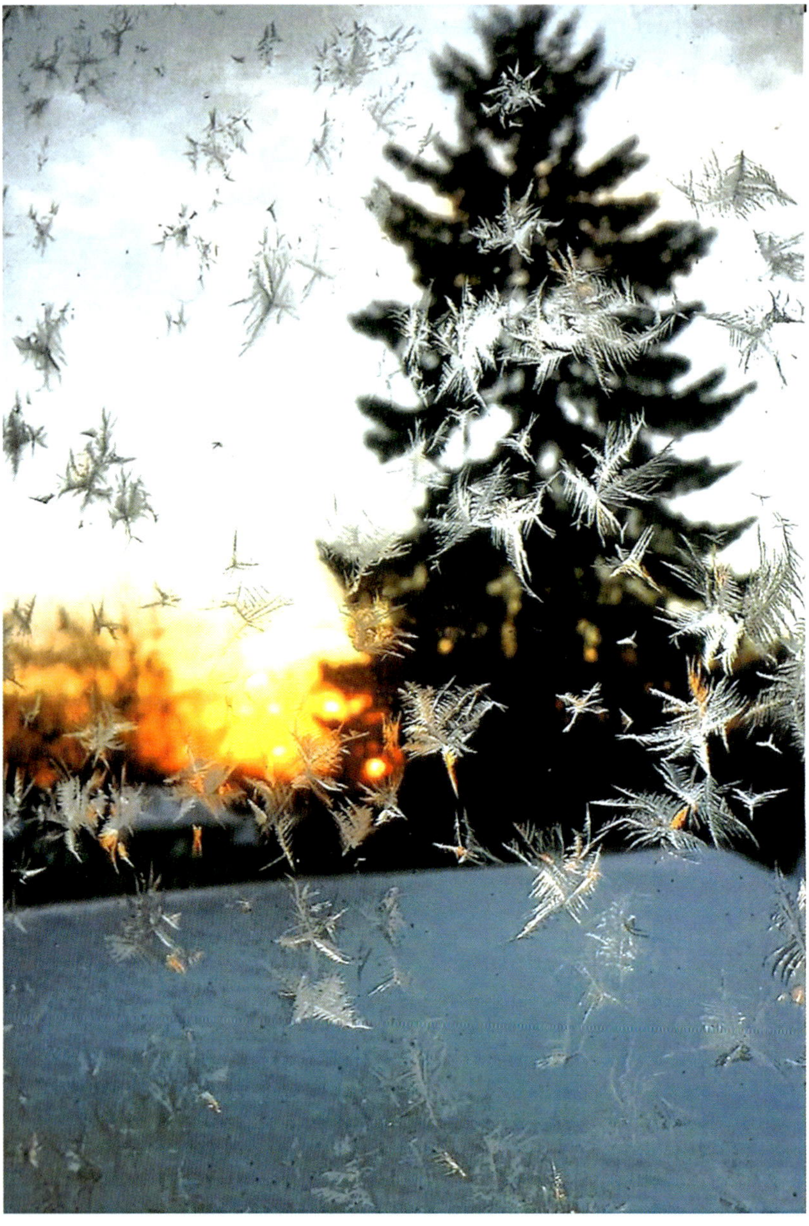

Journey To Earth

Quiet snowflakes, drift softly in my mind,
Mesmerizing...tranquilizing...falling soft and fine....
Blanket my thoughts with peacefulness,
As you cover the earth with snow,
Drifting, sifting, softly lifting...
The spirits of us, below.
Intricate and dainty,
As they're floating thru the air;
Snowflakes softly sifting down...
To cover the trees, so bare.
How much more beauty could there be
Than whiteness all around you...
And not a sound to mar the peace,
Let quietness surround you.
Quilt the ground with flakes of white
And quilt my mind with peace...
Cover the old and barren earth,
Let all my anxiousness cease!
Aren't you quite the same as us,
As you're falling from the sky,
Individual, each flake alone...
'til you reach the ground where you lie.
And then you all look quite the same,
In your blanket of pure, white snow...
It reminds me of us, who compete and fuss
But we're all the same, you know.
Some are loving...some are cold,
Some people have beautiful faces...
But inside, aren't we all alike;
Don't we all have equal graces?
and when we finally reach the end
Of our floating 'round on earth...

• • •

We're all the same,
We all are one...
We all know death and birth.
So, may we see, that as the snow,
You sent us here, put us below...
To live our separate lives, that's true,
But to help each other as we pass through.
The snow that falls will melt and blend...
And so will people, in the end...
Our lives no longer will separate be,
They'll all be one life,
One with thee.

Countless Blessings

To travel the world is delicious
And live like a king or a queen...
And with all of this beauty around me,
I am thankful, for all that I've seen.

For I now have more depth and awareness...
Of this beauteous world God has made,
His blessings as countless as shells on the shore
With this breath taking beauty, I prayed;

"I thank You for ears that can hear the roar,
Of the waters that splash on the sand...
For waters that go on forever, as this,
Were not made by the whim of a man,"

The ocean is awesome; has power,
I smiled as I walked in the tide...
And I said, "thank God I have eyes to see,"
And God's presence I felt by my side.

I will never forget you, my ocean...
You are all that I dreamed of and more,
So I drink in your beauty and store it away
As I take one last glance, from your shore!

First Visit to "My" Ocean

You laugh when I call it, "My Ocean,"
As if it were solely for me...
But the fact that's so grand and magnificent,
Is we all can possess it, you see!

Because when you look at "the" ocean...
You realize beyond any doubt,
That "the" ocean's so huge, so expansive...
Well you know what I'm talking about.

It's for you...It's for me...It's for all men...
It's a gift to be given away,
You can say it is yours, I can say it is mine,
But there's still water left on display!

You can love it...possess it and call it your own,
For it somehow just makes it more dear...
So, now that I've told you the way that I feel...
Has "My" ocean become now- more- clear?

FOAMY LACE

TO TASTE THE SALT UPON YOUR LIPS,
TO RUN BAREFOOT, IN THE SAND...
TO FEEL THE POWER OF THE WAVES,
HOLD A STARFISH IN YOUR HAND...
TO DRINK THE BEAUTY THAT YOU SEE,
MORE THAN A HEART CAN HOLD...
TO RUN AND LAUGH UPON THE SHORE,
TO HAVE JOY THAT CAN'T GROW OLD...
TO FEEL THE SUN, WARM ON YOUR BACK,
THE WIND UPON YOUR FACE...
TO WATCH YOUR FOOTPRINTS IN THE SAND,
DISAPPEAR IN FOAMY LACE.
TO FEEL EXCITEMENT, DEEP WITHIN,
THAT PENETRATES YOUR SOUL...
TO BE AWARE...TO BE ALIVE...
TO FEEL COMPLETELY WHOLE!
TO HAVE THIS SPECIAL MEMORY,
OF GREAT BEAUTY LOCKED AWAY,
INSIDE MYSELF...TO FEAST UPON,
'TIL I RETURN, SOMEDAY!

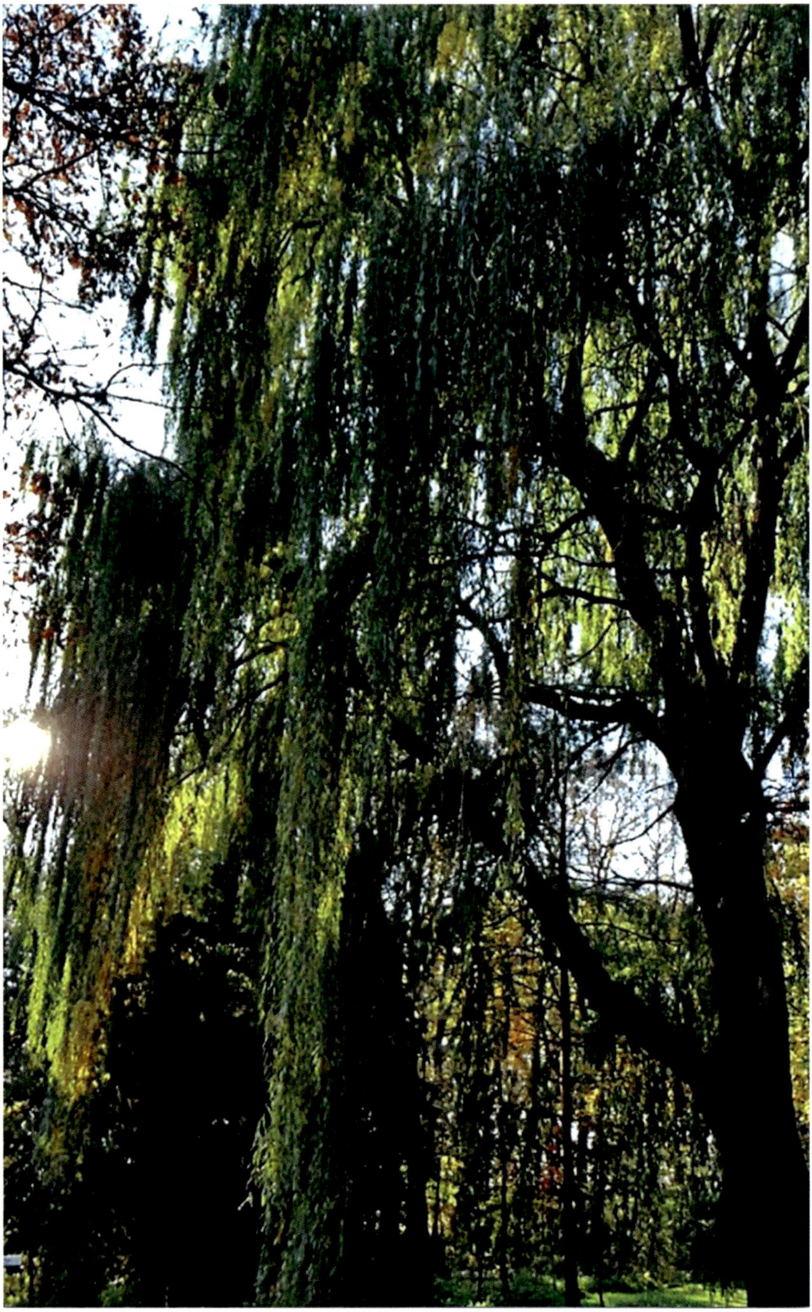

Willow Weeping

From my slumber, sound and deep
I was awakened from my sleep
A roaring sound just filtered in
Which I determined, was the wind.
I ran to the window in time to see
Then cried, "there goes our willow tree!"
As it cracked and hit the ground
Its branches scattered all around
The wind relentless, trees bowed low
They almost kissed the earth...
But stood their ground for all their worth.
But not the willow; gnarled and old
Its time was done, its story told
It held our swing for years and years
I sat beneath and dried my tears
When mother died, it gave me rest
Beneath its branches, I de-stressed.
Although twisted, gnarled, old and bare
When in bloom it looked so fair!

...

It held our hammock in it too,
Lying there seeing skys of blue
Rocking gently in the breeze
Doze a little, if you please!
It spread its shade from too much sun
The umbrella of leaves covered everyone
It kept us cool, when days were hot
Its shelter made the perfect spot!
It seemed appropriate to me
That night as I ran out to see
I watched it go, I saw it fall
Now on the ground, a willow wall.
I let out a gasp, AND THEN a sigh…
As I STOOD AND watched my willow die.
For 30 years I loved that tree
And I believe that it loved me!
It solidly stood to guard the shore
Not only for 30 but so many more!
Now only the stump stands, that is all
Goodbye my willow, you took the fall
And thru the years, you blessed us all!

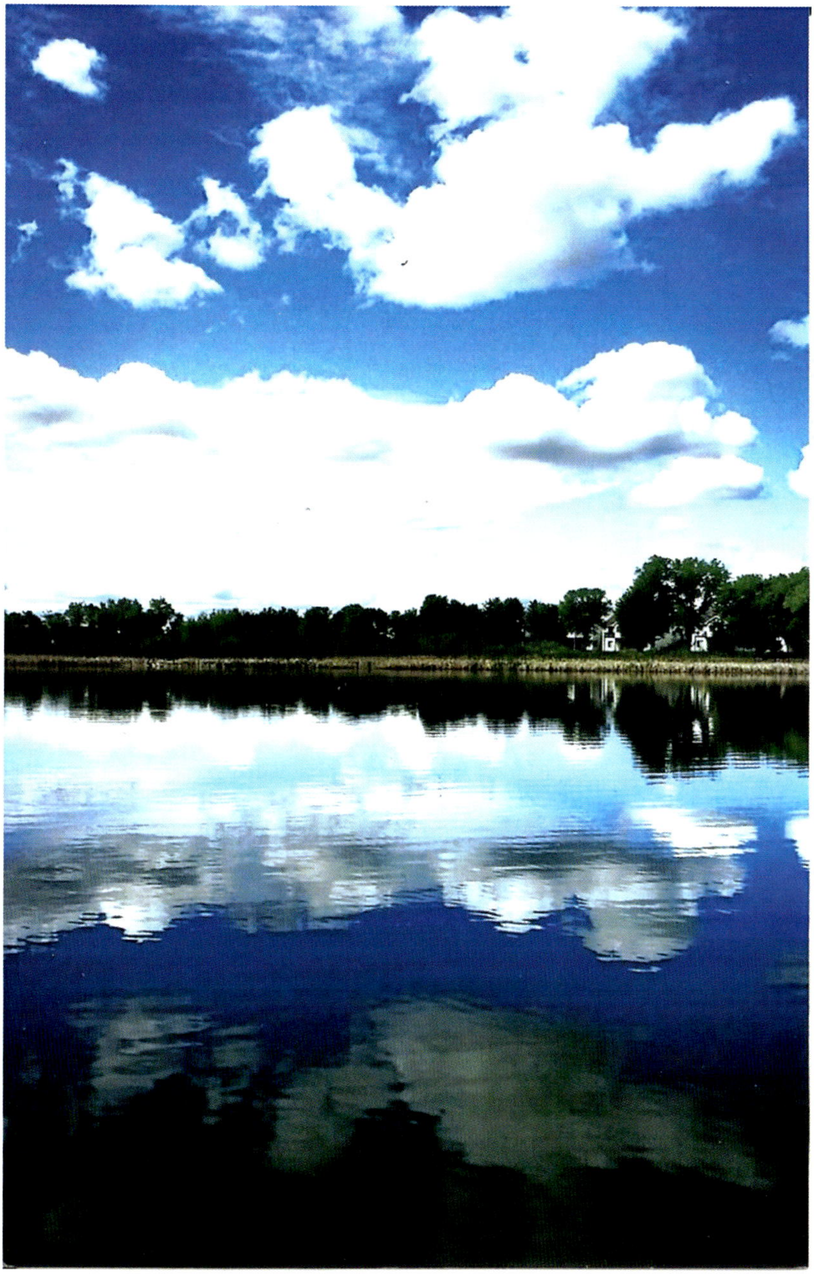

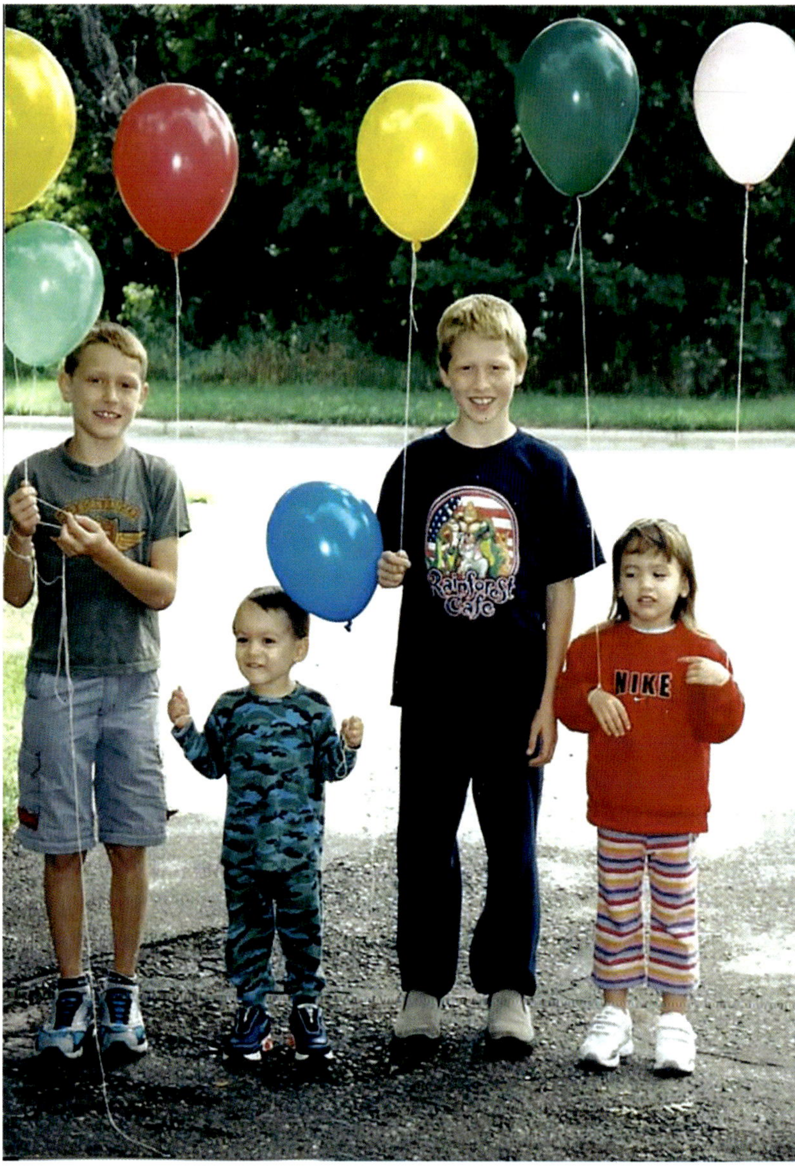
Rainforest Cafe
NIKE

CHAPTER FOUR
Family

Childhood Thoughts

Growing up with five sisters and one brother;
My big sister, Dianne Karen, six years older than me was my idol.
I tried everything I could to be just like her…from stealing her clothes while she was gone (then carefully and quickly hanging them back in her closet while still warm from my body heat and perfume) to playing her albums on her stereo and smoking cigarettes with her and writing letters to boyfriends, late at night, with curlers in our hair, of course.
We went to church together in our chapel veils. I used her precious Tony Doll anytime she would let me or would leave the house ☺
I tried anything I could to grow up…just like her.
Then she left for Nurses training, far away, in Mitchell South Dakota, and wow, my life was sure empty without her!

My only and older big Brother, Gary Robert, was surely my hero growing up. He chased away the boys on the school playground who were chasing me and pulling my pony tail or trying to kiss me. We took hikes together down to the Falls and Minnehaha Creek….
we ate picnic lunches outside together and even dragged a humongous snapping turtle, full of worms, home from the falls, in a cardboard box, for Grandma to make her famous (he said) turtle soup for us…he insisted! Even as we crossed the creek on stones and my stone "moved,"
He yelled, "keep on it," it's a huge turtle, not a stone, and we'll bring it home for supper…as I floated down the creek!

● ● ●

Then he crept over to where some workers were eating their
lunch and dumped out their lumber and stole the box to carry
the turtle home in. It was heavy and we walked a few miles!
Needless to say, our Dad brought it down to the river
after work and let it go…..no soup tonight!
He also had cute boyfriends he brought home and
it was fun to flirt with them.
When he left for the service I missed him terribly!
When he would call home, long distance,
we all waited on the stairs to say a word or two to him.

My little sister, Mary Elise, a cute little blonde,
who squeezed our hamster 'til it peed because it was so cute…
and used to dig her fingernails into our Christmas candy
to see what kind it was…and bit my Uncle Tom in the leg
then smiled to look innocent….was a hoot!

Then came my sister, Linda Lee, who had pretty brown hair
and pouty lips. Quiet, little Linda, who stood all through
one dinner because she wouldn't ask for a stool to sit on
and no one knew she was standing. She and Mary were almost
"book-end" twins, born 13 months apart and were inseparable!
When I started to earn money from babysitting or a rare allowance,
I always went to Woolworths store and bought them
matching outfits and put their hair in braids or pony tails.

• • •

Then along came blue-eyed Jeanne Marie,
whose gorgeous curly hair looked, (as my Aunt Audie
said when she was born) like it was combed with
an egg beater! She was my little dolly. I took her everywhere,
walked her in the buggy, read to her and played with her
like my own dolly.

And, at last, came baby Roberta Joanne, named after my father.
Our little, dark eyed cutie pie, another dolly for me to hold
and play with and dress in darling clothes.
She had a favorite stuffed monkey she held all the time
so she was my little, monkey baby! I was a very proud
big sister to them! I wanted to buy them everything
I could and read to them and care for them!

So this was my world, growing up,
how blessed I was then and now…
and I thought I'd share these precious thoughts of family.

SPREADING SUNSHINE

THERE WAS A GIRL WHO LEFT
A LITTLE SUNSHINE EVERYWHERE,
A LITTLE GIRL WHO SMILED...
AS IF SHE NEVER HAD A CARE!
SHE SMILED AT THOSE WHO HAD A FROWN;
AND THOSE WHO SEEMED QUITE GRUMPY...
SHE SMILED STILL, AT ALL SHE KNEW,
EVEN WHEN "HER" ROAD WAS BUMPY!

SHE BAKED AND BAKED CUPCAKES FOR ALL!
JUST TO SEE THEM SMILE...
AND GAVE HER TIME UNSELFISHLY,
SHE WALKED THE EXTRA MILE!
SHE SPREAD HER "HAPPINESS" AROUND...
FROM KID TO KID AND TOWN TO TOWN
HER DOCTORS AND HER NURSES TOO
THE TEACHERS AND TO ALL SHE KNEW.

A DAY-BRIGHTENER WAS WHAT SHE'D SHARE...
TO TAKE AWAY THEIR WORRIED CARE;
GOOEY, YUMMY, SUGAR SWEET!!!
SHE'D ALWAYS BE THERE WITH A TREAT!
SHE'LL NEVER KNOW HOW LIVES WERE BRIGHTER...
CARES WERE FORGOTTEN, BURDENS LIGHTER!
SHE'LL NEVER KNOW IF ONE WAS "DOWN"
HOW HER SWEETNESS TURNED THEIR FROWN
INTO A SMILE & BLESSED THEIR DAYS,
WITH ALL HER SWEET & CARING WAYS!!!
SENDING KISSES IN THE WIND, CATCH THEM THEY ARE FREE...
AND I'M SENDING LOTS OF LOVE TO MY LISAMARIE.

She Gives Her All

There was a little girl... who loved her mama so...
She tried, in every way she knew, to let her mama know!

So when her birthday came along...even though "spare-time" was rare...
She ran and ran and shopped and shopped and spent without a care!

For everything she saw, she knew would make her mama smile;
She grabbed and paid and tucked away....
To save it for a while.

Until her Mama's special day, her birthday came along...
And then this girl was happy...as she sang the birthday song!

She just couldn't give enough... because her heart was big and kind,
So she just gave "everything" she had...and didn't even mind!

She stood beside her mama as they sang the birthday song
And sang with all her might...oh yes...she really sang along!

• • •

She shares her time and life and love
Reflections of the Father, above
Although she's small her heart is huge and generous, indeed
Don't tell her what you want...she'll give you everything you need!

And more and more and more and more she'll fill you to the brim
With gifts and love and food and warmth...and flash you a big grin!

So here's my thanks, my little girl, you fill my heart with glee...
I can't even begin to say how much you mean to me!
So here's my love and thanks and hugs for all you say and do...
My "little" girl...I'll end with this...oh, Bridgee, I love you!!!

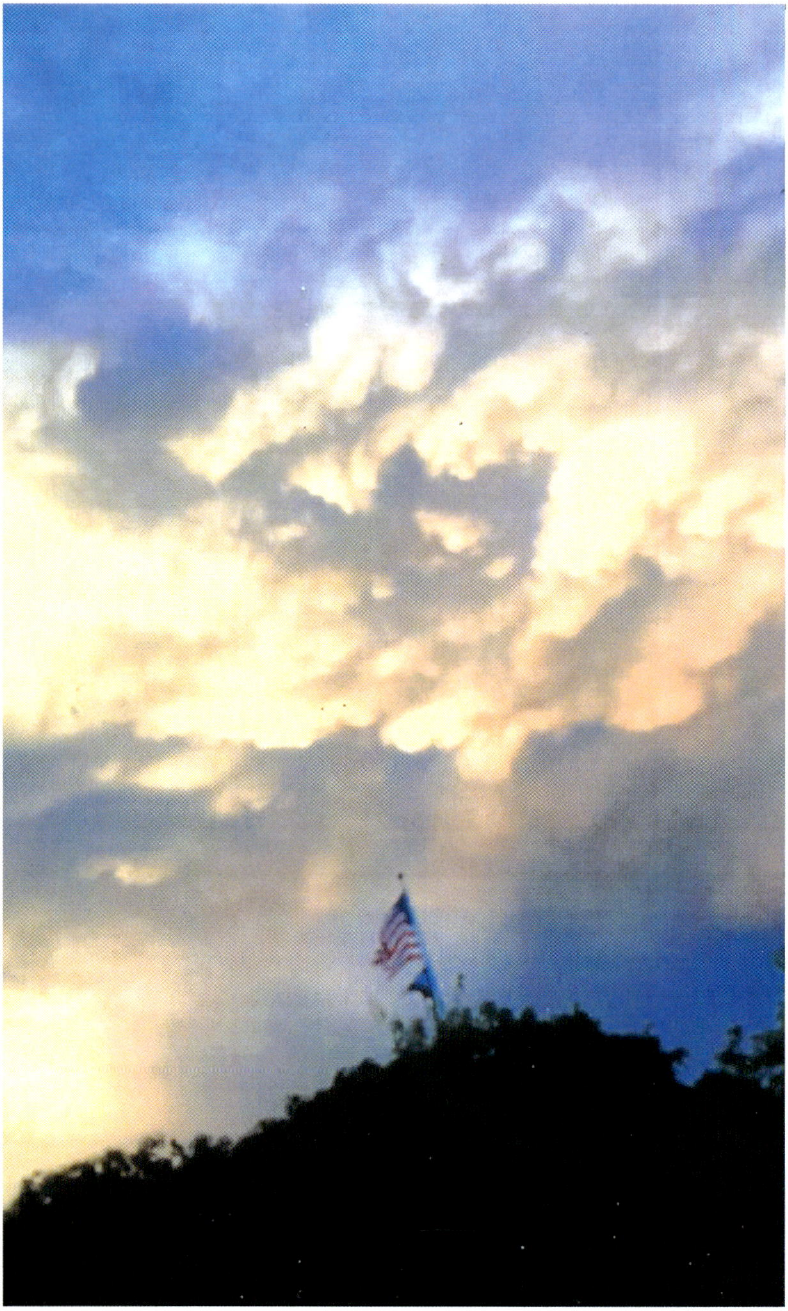

The 4th of July, 2007

The "2007" picnic is through,

We couldn't have done it without all of you!

Just as I thought, "I can't do this alone,"

You sprang into action, as I stifled a groan!

The oceans of salad and food WILL be served

You jumped into "catering mode" and spoke not a word!

And, suddenly, the food was out,

And all arranged, without a doubt!

Our "Daughter and Sister crew" came through again…

"We'll feed this crew, oh yes, we can!"

Then, as I turned around to run

A twinkling man smiled wide, in fun…

"A pontoon driver, perhaps, you need?"

I smiled and happily agreed!

"Oh, yes, please, would you? Idea's great."

The pontoon was sitting there, big, dead weight.

So, all in all, the day was fun,

The food was served, the boats were run;

The "65" who came to play,

And gather, as family, that sunny day…

Each one left with a memory inside…

Of our family reunion, celebrated with pride!

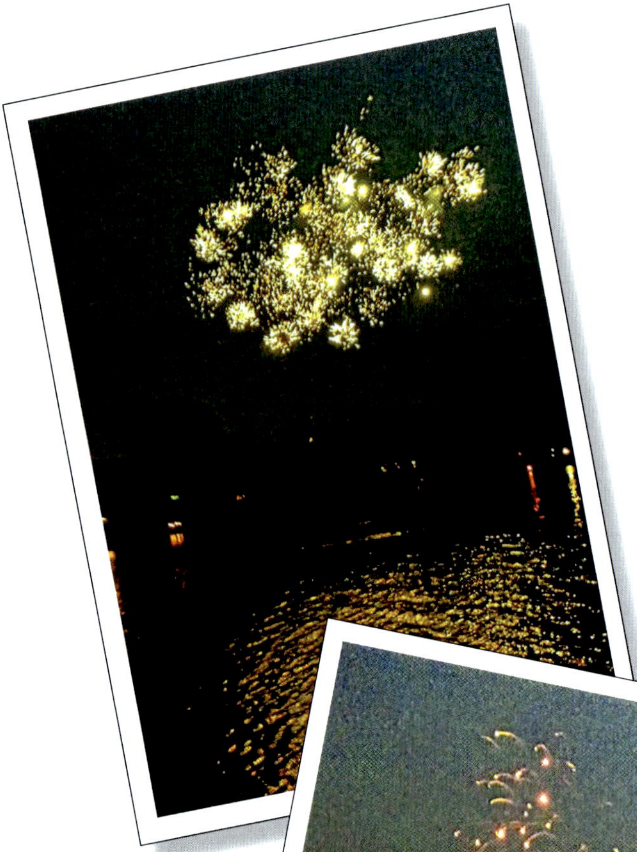

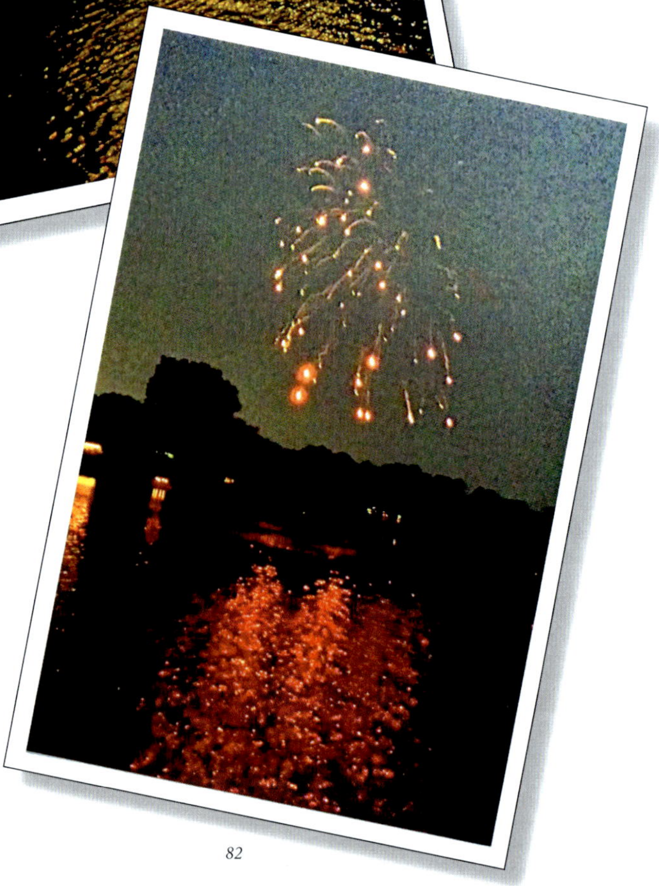

The 4th of July, 2009

Our 4th went fine, 2009, was beautiful, as ever
Until a cloud burst and a wind became the current weather!
It blew on through, as we watched and stood,
But stopped, it did, we prayed it would!
Jack and Soph danced in the rain,
And other children too…they all got soaked
But then, I bet, they really, hardly knew!
Cuz then jumped right into the lake…
A swim, a dive, they thought they'd take!
It all dried out, no harm was done,
The day was good and lots of fun!
Water sports and pontoon rides,
And volley-ball and down the slide!
Good food was served, desserts were too
Talk and laughter all a-brew!
Our 2nd year without our Mom…
But true to her, we traveled on!
For ties are close and family dear
Her spirit was especially near.
Our children helped us to prepare
Without their help, we wouldn't dare!
And, everyone brought delicious dishes
The food was great, beyond all wishes!

• • •

*The dusk then fell, the night had come,
I breathed a prayer to God, to Mom,
And said, "I'll see you, in the moon,
We feel you here, you left too soon!
But now, you have a front-row seat
For fireworks! And your life's complete!"
I could just hear you,
"Ahhhhh and UUUUUUU…"
And feel you smiling, as they flew;
The moon so full, the fireworks grand
I could almost feel your hand…
In mine, so soft, so warm, so like it was
A short, short time ago…
Happy 4th, my little Mom, I truly love you so!*

Tears Over a Cheese Sandwich

Only a Mom could possible know
His favorite sandwich, that he loves so...
Only the heart of a Mom could tell
Could read in his eyes
Could know, so well;
What matters to this little man,
What he can't take and what he can!
Moms just know...with words "unspoken,"
When their child's heart is broken!
Moms can touch and Moms can feel
Their child's desires...which are so real.
And, so, Moms want the very best
And for their children they stand the test!
And weary and tired, though night grows late,
Those clean clothes and lunches
just cannot wait!
The extra note, tucked in with love
Adds a pinch of heaven from above!
And now and then, throughout his day
He feels her warmth in a special way.
Cuz Mommy's love is always there...to hug,
to love, to always care!
So through our care, concern and love,
We grace our Father, up above;
And we are blessed, beyond compare,
Far more than any words can tell
With him, our child, we love so well!

Kisses

Throwing kisses, in the wind,
From one state to another...
Says my Daughter, on the phone,
"I hope you catch them, Mother!"

Though hundreds of miles
Span the gap
Between her house and mine;
Our interwoven hearts might stretch
But will never break the bind!

The bind that ties us,
Heart to heart...
No matter that we're far apart,
Throwing each other a hug and a kiss
That Daughter of mine
That I so miss!!!

We share our "cuppa" on the phone
So neither one will feel alone.
Throwing kisses on the phone,
From one state to another,
While trying to smile...
We hold back tears,
A Daughter and her Mother!

. . .

Here's a kiss
And here's a prayer...
I send them floating thru the air;
In hopes your angel's wings are strong
To place them right where they belong!

XO catch!

My Heart is Blessed

I sold a house today, to my Sister and her Husband.

They were in their house 16 years, a pillar throughout turmoil...

I am happy for them, I am drained.

When I came home tonight,

Our oldest Grandson picked a fresh, tiny, white flower and put it in my hand...

And he gave me a rock from the lake,

And a very big hug and a kiss.

I am rich, beyond compare!

Our Daughter came by and surprised us with her new 7 week old puppy,

She is as a new Mom, protective and loving

And, very, very happy!

I am rich, beyond compare!

My wealth exceeds any expectations

My heart is blessed

My God is very near, in the presence of this Day!

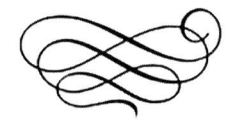

Sweet Blessings in Life;
"Siblings"

S iblings love you,
W hen others walk away!
E ven during hard times;
E ver at your side.
T hey think the same as you do.
        And...

B elieve in you...
L eave you laughing...
E xcellent listeners...
S well buddies...In
S unshine and shade! They are:
I nstrumental in your success!
N ever forgetting to razz you as you
G o along life's way...They add a
S weetness that no one else can!

I mpossible to ignore!
N ever changing in their steadfastness.

L eading the way & lighting your path
I nstead of waiting for someone else to come along...
F aithful prayer partners...
E ncouraging your love of God.

S illy, random laughs,
I nsane jokes!
B uilds your confidence...
L istens with their hearts...
I gnores your faults...
N ever gives up on you!
G ives selflessly...
S hines forever in your heart!

      (I am blessed with **SIX!**)

A Little Valentine

She fell asleep…a-top her bed
The over-head light shone bright…
Her valentines spread all around…
She was so tired tonight!
She wrote each one…each X and O
And maybe a little verse,
And, finally, after all this day
They were properly disbursed!
Her Grandkids "ooo'd and ahhh'd"
And hugged their Grandma so…
For all the fun and love she brought,
And begged her not to go!
A couple other stops she made
Before this day was through
A Daughter and a Sister
With her loving wishes too.
A valentine, to show her love
Her Sister, she would bring…
Which truly made her day
A caring, precious thing!
Now on to see her Daughter too
Though it was late…away she flew!
Another hug to pass along
Her generous heart was like a song!

• • •

She made them all feel warm and cozy
But now she was feeling a little dozy...
So when she finally saw that bed
She never even turned down the spread!
Sleep tight and rest..you deserve the best.
Sunshine you've spread..now, jump into bed!
Before she knew, she was fast asleep
A candy heart lay at her feet...
Sleep tight, you little valentine
You always show your love, so fine!

*A new command I give you: Love one another.
As I have loved you, so you must love one another.
By this everyone will know that you are my disciples,
if you love one another.
John 13:34-35*

Snowflake

Three baby squirrels fell... "flop" to the ground!
And, as both of us saw...
There was no "Mama" around.
Snowflake, the white squirrel fell out of the tree;
Who came to the rescue?
Yup! Jeanne Marie!

She thought she would put them safely in a box...
So, outside she ran; in her shoes and her socks!
Over she leaned, thinking they must be dead;
Falling so hard and right on their heads!
Just ready to gently put them away,
"a CHATTER... a SCREACH..."
She jumped...she should not stay!

Along came the "Mama" from where I can't say...
Picking each one up, firmly,
And then ran away!

*Now, Jeanne Marie keeps
those baby squirrels fed
They just sit on her chair
and eat all her white bread!
As she opens the door,
with the bread in her hand...
This fat, little, Snowflake,
is at her command!*

*She's "goetten," herself
a pet squirrel you see...
It's Snowflake, a white one,
For Jeanne Marie!*

SNOWBABY SISTER

SNOWBABY SISTER, YOU JUMP TOO HIGH!
SO HUG ME TIGHT OR WE MIGHT FLY...

SNOWBABY SISTER, LET'S LAUGH AND FALL,
SO WE WON'T HAVE ANY CARES AT ALL!

SNOWBABY SISTER, MY WONDERFUL FRIEND,
I COUNT THE TIMES JOYOUS THAT TOGETHER WE SPEND!

SNOWBABY SISTER, YOU'RE PRECIOUS, YOU'RE DEAR,
I'M SENDING A HUG, MAY IT LAST ALL YEAR!

(Written after some high-flying fun on the kid's trampoline)

You Are You

You are you and I am Me
I think we should go climb a tree...
We may have peace, up in the air,
And swing our feet without a care.
And ring the bell to let mom know
We're ready for "the bucket" soooooo...

Hey wait; you were the one up there
Laughing and without a care!
I was the one who helped mom bring
That bucket filled with everything!!

Hey, how come?...
did you have fun??

Love, your older Sister

(Remembering our maple tree fun in the summer...
when Mom would bring us all treats in the bucket
with a rope attached to it and we would pull it up, Dad included)

Memories Unforeseen

Some of the mundane tasks we do
Carry with them memories strong & true.
A linen cabinet to be cleaned
Filled with reminders, unforeseen.
A pretty towel that's still brand new;
Given by Mom especially to you...
At least 8 years ago, must be
With her handwritten note
Pinned on, I see:
"love you, hugs and kisses too,"
Her memory warms me, thru and thru!
In a pillow case, now I find...
Crocheted pot holders, the homemade kind,
His Mom placed gently in my hand,
And said, "take these," you understand;

I stacked some in a pile to put away...
When my Husband came in, I had to say...
"remember these? They're hand crocheted,
made by your Mom and done so well!"
He picked them up and breathed in their smell...
With glistening eyes...he held them close
"they smell like Mom's perfume,
Almost!"
Yes, loving memories linger still
I pray to God they always will!
The treasures that they left on earth;
Are priceless, far beyond their worth

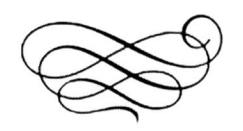

Who Is That In The Mirror?

My skin's getting wrinkled, she says in dismay
My memory's fading, my hair's turning gray!
How could this happen, in such a short time?
Why, wasn't it yesterday I was in my prime?

I forgot what I entered this room to find…
Sometimes I feel completely out of my mind!
At times I can't hear you, are you talking too fast?
I admit that my stories are all in the past.
My Children are grown up,
The Grandchildren too…
But I can remember when they were so new.
I glance in the mirror,
An old lady stares back…
She looks vaguely familiar
It's just youth that she lacks!

My whole life's been a dance
That I'd not want to miss…
And I'm in my last chapter,
It's come down to this.
It's been good, it's been fine
And I gave it my all…
At times standing strong,
Other times I would fall.

• • •

But I lived and I loved
And I danced every dance,
And I didn't go under…
With bad circumstance!

I am proud of my Family,
I am proud of my life…
I loved being a Mother, a Sister, a Wife.
A Gramma, an Auntie, a Friend to a few,
Who, even in tough times,
Remained always "true blue."

Through A Child's Eyes

He built things sturdy, as he built them strong,
With unceasing determination...
And there wasn't a hurricane forceful enough
To blow down my Father's creations.

A child's world, when you're very small,
Is no wider than your own back yard...
And my Father used sweat, not money,
For his family he worked very hard!

And my little eyes watched,
As I played and he worked...
And erected a swing set so tall,
That a giant could swing
(standing up, I suppose)
Without hitting his head, once, at all!

Though I was a very small, little girl,
I knew he could lift the whole earth!
My girlfriends and all of our neighbors knew that
You could tell he gave all he was worth.

He laid down a sidewalk
(was nothing to him)
And he built a sandbox, mighty fine!
He put each of our handprints on one of the sides
And our prints, at that time, numbered nine.

• • •

And, he was our King, our protector, our God.
Yes, God is the word I must use...
Now I realize I thought he was stronger than life.
And, if death came around, he'd refuse.

And I remember feeling angry
At my Father when he died...
How dare he leave us all alone?
Mom had no one at her side.

When anger left me; I felt a shock.
That chilled me to the bone...
Not one of us really has a choice.
It's God's will....All His own.

We choose not how or when we'll die.
But how to LIVE each day...
How to be strong and how to love.
And help along the way.

Well, I'll tell ya this, from within my heart.
God must have needed him too...
He must have been building a castle of brick
And knew Dad would see it through.

He's building it sturdy, as he's building it strong.
The best creation he's ever made.
For he knows his family needs somewhere to live
When our dues, in this life, have been paid.

My Plea

I asked for a furnace to keep them warm
And give them repose,
From the bitter life's storm...
And, God said, "Yes, a furnace is fine,
But the warmth that they need
Is of much greater kind!"
I asked for a house
To protect them from harm...
And God said, "The lesson is,
Don't be alarmed...
For when life sends it's blows
And you're beaten and worn,
You must never give up
Or feel lost or forlorn!"
"For the warmth and protection
That I have in mind...
Is of infinite graces,
The much greater kind!"
They will warm you
Right down to the tips of your toes...
And, this thing that you ask for,
HE already knows.

...

Trust and pray and listen and know...
Your heavenly Father loves you so!
His plan is greater than we can see...
He knows the way and cares for me!
Trust and believe and walk ahead
It is not our lot
To be filled with dread.
For, how can we praise Him
With hearts downcast?
He never will fail us,
His love will last!

*(Written at a low time when a loved one and her babies
didn't have a furnace or the funds to get one......
God provided one shortly thereafter and HE threw in a house too)*

*The Lord is the one who goes ahead of you;
He will be with you. He will not fail you or
Forsake you. Do not fear or be dismayed.
Deuteronomy 31:8*

Encouragement From Beyond

While sorting through her things one day,
My Siblings all around...
Among the magazines stacked there,
Old calendars, I found...
I couldn't let them just be thrown,
For within each day...
Her thoughts were known.
Her dear hand-written dates and times,
Were neatly spaced within the lines.
And, now and then, a weather brief...
"today too hot," next day, "relief."
It was as if she were still here...
Penning her schedule, that little dear.
The ache of loneliness inside me
As I read each word, as if to guide me.
Made me weak with grief, still fresh...
I miss her more, not any less!
I miss her more, as time goes by,
And ache so much, at times I cry.
Soon we will have "sorted through"
All the things my Mother knew.

Soon we will be done, you see,
Her treasures divided equally.
We shall carry thru what she had said,
And when cards and notes have all been read
Her dishes gone thru...one by one
With memories of our childhood fun.
We will, then still, have one another,
And forever and ever, our sweet Mother!

Ps, we're still finding little notes
Cut out with pinking shears,
And lots of coins and dollars too,
Hidden away, because she knew...
One day...after she was gone,
We'd find her encouragement
From beyond!

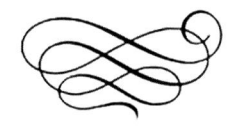

The Heart of a Woman...

Strong...
My heart beats strong...
The heart of a woman...
A Mother...A Sister...A Friend...A Gramma
A woman's heart beats on...

I sweep up the last of the crumbs and crumbles underneath their
chairs that they always sit at;
I almost hate to throw them away,
it will be a long time until I sweep up their crumbs again.

Strong...
My heart beats strong...
The heart of a woman...
A Mother...A Sister...A Friend...A Gramma
A woman's heart beats on...

I wash their sheets and blankets and pick up some
long, black strands of her hair...
a candy wrapper in a corner of the bedroom where he slept...

• • •

I put the lilacs in a glass vase and smell the lilacs she picked and put
on her cupboard as she cleaned her house for the last time…
she brought them here to our house…
they were sweet…almost sickeningly sweet, for they meant goodbye…
like the perfume she always wore, "Eternity"…
it will seem so, to not see her……an eternity.
I find a rock that says, "Remember," lying on the bedroom floor.
After dropping them off at the airport the reading for that day
is all about Jesus, our Rock…

Strong…
My heart beats strong…
The heart of a woman…
A Mother…A Sister…A Friend…A Gramma
A woman's heart beats on…

Why does it?
How does it?
Why doesn't it stop beating?
My heart beats strong…

Before she leaves for a new home in a new state she calls,
"Gramma!!! Come here please…"
I go swiftly up the stairs…
she hands me two different candies…"I can't take these on the plane,…
my Mom says,…will you save them for me? I WILL be coming back!"
Then the jar containing her "Oscar the caterpillar,"…
whom she's been feeding all week…and giving drops of water to…
"Gramma, give wormy his freedom, at your house, will you please?"
Her big, brown eyes gaze into mine… "Please, Gramma…
I can't take him on the plane."

Strong…
My heart beats strong…
The heart of a woman…
A Mother…A Sister…A Friend…A Gramma
A woman's heart beats on…

• • •

I am saving all my money and allowance to send you
a round-trip plane ticket, Gramma…to come for my 14th Birthday."
Our Grandson says, "I'll see you when I get to Heaven someday,
Gramma…" They both cry saying goodbye to their friends at school…
their "relationships" as he says… We invite the friends over
to swim together for the last time…it's freezing out…
but they all jump into the lake together anyway…and eat hot dogs
and laugh until we almost die!!!

Their Mom walks thru a now-empty house…
each room again and again…and Gramma does too…
(bathrooms are for hiding in and crying)…

We all go to the kids concerts at school one last time…
when it's over we take pictures…we stand around…
no one wanting to leave for the last time…it feels like a funeral…
a wake…it feels sad…finally, as they go to close the school…
we all walk outside but we still just stand there…

It's not like they're dead or anything…why be so sad?…
no more crumbs…no more giggling…
no more staying up late together…
no more jokes…no more cookies:)…
no more "storming" in the door…
no more school concerts, or plays, no more…
seeing them grow up…
no more chicken fried rice; he taught me how to make it
but mine doesn't taste as good…
no more razzing and teasing and such;
They're too far away and my heart hurts so much!

Strong…
My heart beats strong…
The heart of a woman…
A Mother…A Sister…A Friend…A Gramma
A woman's heart beats on…

• • •

I take more pictures, make albums, trying to capture
every moment together...every bug they catch, every tear they cry...
every joke they make up...every time we laugh until we cry...
The dropping-in numerous times a week is done now...
she won't be at the door...only perhaps maybe one time a year...
maybe or maybe not...
Email, snap chat, tango, instagram, texting, phone calls,
face book, snail mail, old-fashioned letters; it's called "change"...
I'm supposed to be open to it...change...
But my heart's the same old heart I always had...

Strong...
My heart beats strong...
The heart of a woman...
A Mother...A Sister...A Friend...A Gramma
A woman's heart beats on...

she calls me crying...it's just a "house" she says...
some of her stuff is lost, some dishes broken, lots of boxes...
I can't hug her...I can't help her unpack...I can't picture her
in her new house... I haven't seen it yet...she's grown up now...
a woman with a woman's heart...
but I still see her as a little child...My little child...afraid...
looking to me for strength...still she is grown...
she has children of her own...

• • •

I go to the store and while checking out I hear, "Grandma!!!"
and I turn...looking for them...wildly happy I turn...
my heart aches as I see children with their own Grandmother,
shopping...smiling...holding her hand in theirs....
It's too soon..................
I keep hearing them, smelling them, seeing them;
it will always be too soon!

Strong...
My heart beats strong...
The heart of a woman...
A Mother...A Sister...A Friend...A Gramma
A woman's heart beats on...

(Our Daughter and her family moved to another
State... We love you and miss you guys!)

"Wren and Lilacs"
Original oil painting by Dianne Goetten Krause

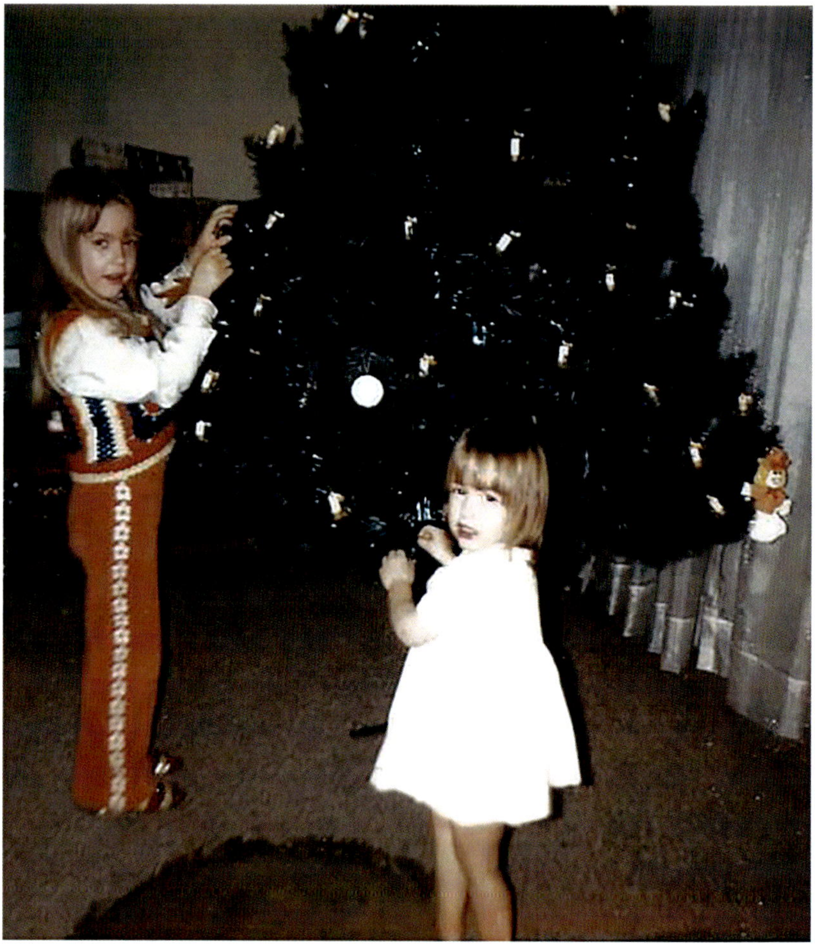

CHAPTER FIVE
Christmas

Tender Little Baby

Tender, little baby...
Our Savior born tonight,
That we may never taste of death
But shall have eternal light!

Holy infant, mild...
We see your brightly shining star,
We shall follow to present ourselves
Exactly as we are!

Radiant, little Christ Child...
We have a room to spare,
Our hearts shall welcome you
With love...
There's room for Jesus there!

So, come, Lord Jesus...
Dwell within,
To you, we sing our praise!
Be born, within our hearts this day
Abide in us...always!

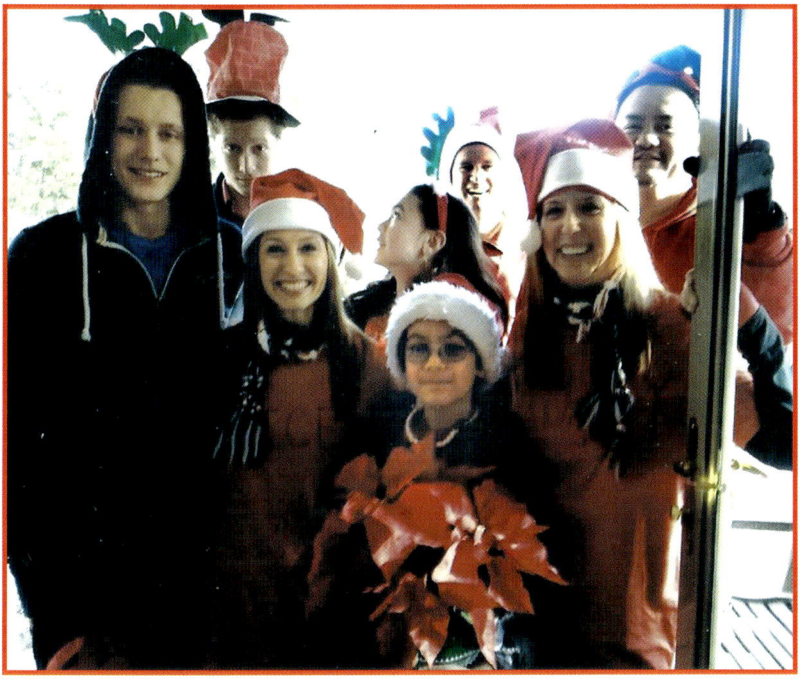

CHRISTMAS IS HERE...HOSANNAS RING

LET HOSANNAS RING IN YOUR HEART...
CHRIST IS BORN; IT'S THE DAY TO START,
BEING KINDER TO YOUR FELLOW MAN...
LET CHRISTMAS LAST AS LONG AS YOU CAN!

LET IT NOT BE FOR ONLY ONE DAY...
MAKE THE SPIRIT LIVE, IN A SPECIAL WAY.
THROUGHOUT THIS YEAR, LET LOVE BE KING...
CHRISTMAS IS HERE HOSANNAS RING.

PRAISE TO THE BABY BORN LONG AGO...
HIS SPIRIT LIVES TODAY, WE KNOW.
LET US REJOICE, LET OUR HEART'S SING...
CHRISTMAS IS HERE HOSANNAS RING!

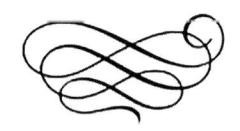

Keeping Christ in Christmas

Let's put Christ back into our Christmas,
Let's change the routine this year…
Let's give Him his place
And honor His name
Let's have a true season of cheer.

Let's pray that "we" will change our world
Starting out first with ourselves…
Take all our selfishness, hatred and greed
And put them all back on the shelves.

Let's place Christ first this Christmas
Then all else will fall into line…
Let's bow our heads and mean that prayer
"not my will, God, but thine!"

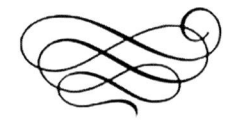

"Angel"
Original oil painting by Dianne Goetten Krause

The Greatest Gift is Love

Another Christmas Eve is here,
The years fly by so fast...
We're gathered 'round our Christmas tree,
We're home again, at last.
Thru the years we come for birthdays,
We celebrate...we sing...
And tonight we come, to honor One,
Whose name is Christ, our King!

This Babe, born so very long ago,
Is born, anew, tonight...
And the loving message His Birthday brings,
Burns warm as candle light.
The Christmas story is very old,
It's been told for centuries...
We hear of kings and shepherd boys,
Who fall down to their knees
And brought their gifts and worshipped,
The little, holy Child...
The One who rules both heaven and earth
This Babe, so sweet and mild.

This eve draws a circle of brotherhood,
'Round our entire earth...
For all who love
And all who praise
Our Blessed Savior's birth.
So let your heart burn warm with love,
Reach out to one another...
As we celebrate, anew, this year,
The birth of Christ, our Brother!

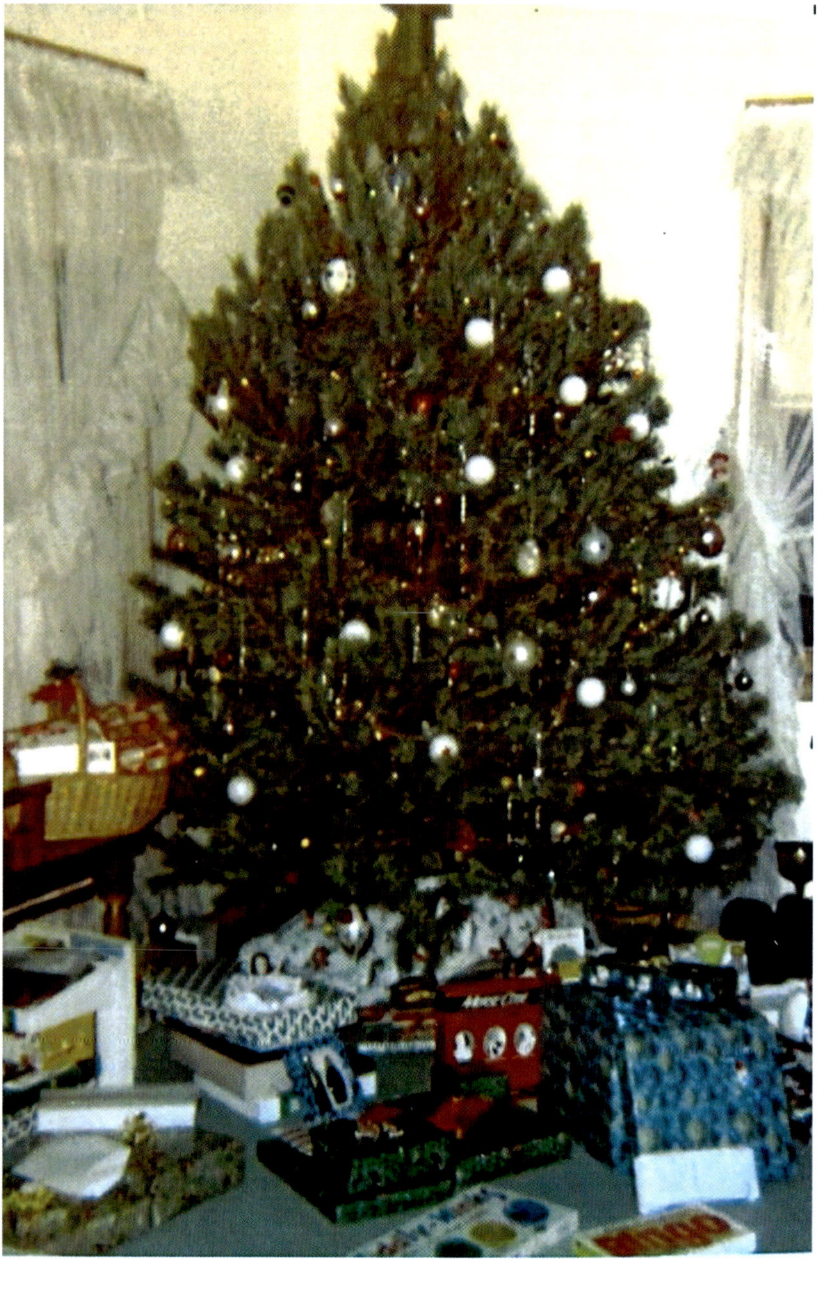

Our Enchanted Christmas

Come wander with me, if you will
And squint your eyes real tight, until…
Once again, it's Christmas time,
And you are very small…
The lights are twinkling, twinkling bright,
You can hardly sleep at all!
Gently falling flakes of snow
A stroll into our past, we go.
Of Christmases so long ago
And seven children, all aglow…
In dreams of lights upon our tree
The fresh pine smell…
The giggling glee…
The sparkling tinsel,
Hung "just so"…
That smell of fresh baked cookies, Ohhh!

Seven kids on seven stairs,
Listening, waiting, breathing prayers
Of special treasures 'neath the tree
That Santa brought for you, for me!
One by one, we woke up Dad
He's finally up; boy, were we glad!

. . .

Every pile stacked, "just the same,"
Toys galore and lots of games.
Fanny Farmer candies passed,
The Goetten Christmas was a gas!
Mogan David wine and Velveeta cheese
Taste a little, if you please...
These treasured memories mean so much
Because of Mother's gentle touch;
A touch of love, of care, of joy,
For their six girls and only boy!

Their secret preparations, we hardly saw or knew
Then suddenly, they all appeared...
As every year we grew.
Her blue eyes...they twinkled,
Her smile...so merry!
Six Daughters, excited...
(and that includes, Gary!)

. . .

We heard his reindeer on our roof
And Dad could always find the proof...
That yes, indeed, his sleigh had come
With treasures now for everyone!

So close your eyes and come along
You can almost hear Mom playing a song...
It's jingle bells and silent night
Her fingers hit those keys "just right!"

Gently falling crystal flakes...
Of puffy, glistening snow...
Relax, enjoy and wander back...
To our Christmas long ago.

Love you guys!

Happy Birthday, Jesus

When I pick out a birthday gift for someone I hold dear
I shop with love and care and hope they treasure it
All year…
I try to find something special, like the one
I'm shopping for…
And when it's bought and wrapped,
I only wish to give them more!

We remember birthdays of those we love the best
And, in December, we celebrate one
More important than all the rest.
The birthday of One who loves us more
Than we can comprehend…
The birthday of One who died for us,
Yet whose life will never end!
This is His Day, His Special Day…
If we love Him with all our heart,
Then we'll wish to celebrate and share
We will want to be a part…
Of His joyous celebration,
Of His birth and of His life…
Then our Christmas season won't be filled
With busyness and strife!

Oh let us reach within our hearts
And ask ourselves today,
Whose birthday we're preparing for
And what does your heart say?

…

If we love Him, as we say we do,
Then what will our gift to Him be?
Something bought and paid for…
That is placed beneath our tree?
Would that gift that you have
Be fit for a King…
If He came right now,
For a visit…
Maybe we'd best unwrap that one,
And look at our gift…what is it?

It should be the best, most loving gift
That ever our hearts could give…
It should be a gift that shows our thanks,
It's because of Him, we live!

What kind of a gift would be fit for a King?
I really cannot say,
Yet I know I must begin, right now…
Prepare for it, today!
I will not sit empty-handed
With no gift beneath my tree,
I will give myself, my heart, my soul…
I will give the Gift of Me!
And, I will strive, in this season of hope,
To be the best person I can
For only the B E S T that is within
Will be fit for the King of Man!

Who or What is Santa Claus?

The little elf sits on a stump and waits for Santa Claus
The older elves tell her he's dumb...
But he believes, because...
Although they say there is no Santa,
That he isn't even real...
This little elf is very wise,
He believes in what he feels!

For all the kind things that you do,
For others, day by day,
Makes Santa Claus as "big as life,"
Quite real, in every way!

Santa is the joy you feel
And the smiles you give another...
And the times she hasn't asked you,
But you've said, "I'll help you, Mother."
Santa means all the thrills and joys
That this old life can hold!
The excitement and the wonder...
You must never get "too old!"

• • •

The twinkle you see in a child's eyes,
On the night before Christ's birth...
And the wonder of waiting for Santa Claus,
Adds joy to this old earth!
And joy must not be stolen,
From a youngster's little mind...
For Santa Claus is warmth and love
And everything that's kind.

So let them laugh at this little elf,
As he sits and waits tonight...
For it's he, who has a happy heart,
And will greet the morning light...
With strong beliefs in goodness,
And a soul so filled with love...
That the Holy Child will send him more,
Than he is dreaming of!

(This was written long ago when my child came to me crying and was told by a friend that there was no Santa)

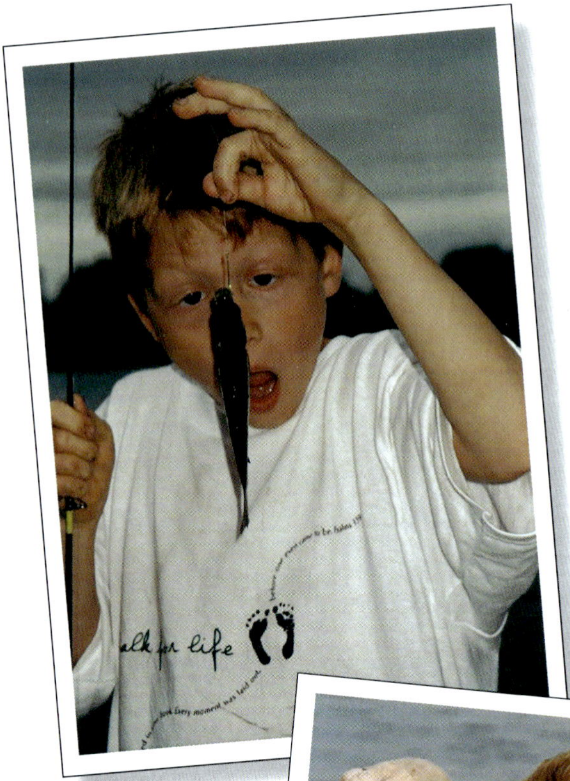
alk for life

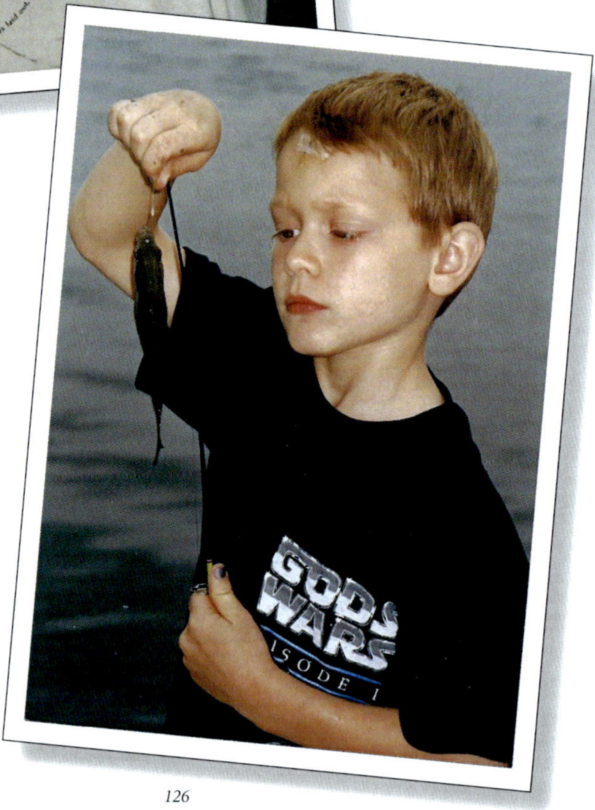
GOD
WARS
ISODE I

CHAPTER SIX
Whimsical Moments of Grandchildren, Fun and Song

I Wish...I Wish...I'd Catch a Fish

"I wish, I wish, I'd catch a fish,"
Said Alexander Paul...
As Matthew James throws in his bread;
"I'm going to catch 'em all!"

Throw in your net go swish, swish, swish,
Then scoop it up...
"I have two fish!"
"Some bread, some worms, is all you need,
These hungry, little fish we'll feed!"

"We'll get 'em, flop...and we won't stop,
We toss 'em back, you see...
And then we catch 'em once again,
A 'lotta fun for you and me!
When Grampa asks, "what did you catch;"

What kind of fish have you?...
I answer back, "He's kinda orange,
And yup, his eyes are blue!"
"I wish, I wish, I'd catch a fish..."
Said Alexander Paul...

And Matthew James throws in his bread,
"I'm gonna catch 'em all!!!"

Sounds "Fishy"

We went to buy a little fish
To put him in our "fish-bowl-dish,"
That's on our dresser, in our home,
But fishy cannot be alone!
And so, we choose another one,
To swim around and have some fun.
Sophie picked one out, with spots;
Jack chose an orange one he liked a lot!
"plop", in the bag with just one swish...
Went our two little golden fish!
But wait! We see another one...
Let's take her too and have some fun.
So that we did, cuz, Mommy said,
And bought some fish food
They must be fed!
We watched our fish.
We liked them lots.
And named them flipper and polka-spots!
And every day, can't wait to see
The orange one that we named, Dorothy!
Swishes, swishes, we love our fishes!

(Soph & Jack, remember your fishes?)

I Won't Be Afraid

If a Big Sea Monster lived in the lake...
I wouldn't be scared, cuz I would just take
Some Oreo cookies and feed them to him;
Then I'd climb on his back and we'd
go for a swim!
And, I would trust him, oh yes, I would,
Because this Big Sea Monster is really so good!
And the bass would follow along behind...
And the Oreo cookies I'd keep to remind...
This Big Sea Monster, that I "really trust,"
That his being good was "really a must!"
He's never would bite, or even be bad...
Cuz the Oreo cookies would keep him so glad!
Even, Myrtle the turtle would scurry away...
As my Big Sea Monster and I were at play!
I would REALLY DO IT, Gramma,
I'd ride on his back!
And I REALLY WOULD TRUST HIM,
I'm telling you that!
So, PLEASE, pack up some cookies
See, look at the clock...
My Sea Monster's waiting
Right there, by the dock!
I REALLY DO TRUST HIM,
I'm going for a ride;
He's happy as long as there's cookies inside!

...

So, Goodbye, but don't worry;

He never does bite!

We won't even go very far from your sight!

I'll hurry right back, you just wait

On the shore...

But, PLEASE, bring those cookies!

I just might need some more!

My Grandson, Alex, tells me this story at bedtime,
after a day on the lake...
"Gramma, make a poem out of it," he says.

I'm Only 4

Goodbye, I'm off to college now...
Our Granddaughter did say,
You can't come with
It's just for kids
And VERY far away!

I have to take a bus or plane,
And pack my bag
What's more...
It's such a LOT for me to do!
You see, I'm only 4!

My teacher gives us SO much work,
We never get a break!
Just every now and then
I'll eat a snack, that I will take!

So, Bye Now, See Ya, Gotta Go!
I'm walking out the door,
I took my lunch to eat at college,
Because I'm only 4!

(Our Granddaughter, Sophie, said this to us at age 4 with her bag packed)

Happy Jack

"Plain ole Gramma, quick, come see!"
His loving eyes shine up at me...
The tiny hand slips into mine
And tugs at me as I recline.

"It's willy pwetty, come on, let's see,
Right over der, behind dat tree.
Can I pick it for my mommy, please?
Der's wots of them beneath the trees!"

Excitement grows...the smile shines,
He's pure delight, Grandson of mine!
For everything is fun and new
The world around him,
Pure and true!

We study bugs, then run away
And giggle, giggle all the day!
His favorite thing is a balloon
Which Grampa will present him, soon.

Grow slowly, slowly, little one
Life is so precious, my Grandson,
And fresh and new and OH so good!
I pray your life forever would
For you be sweet
And always bless
Your little heart with happiness!

"Let's Write a Poem, Gramma"

There's dirt on the rug and sand on the floor;
Dirty dishes are in the sink.
My house is a mess...I don't look so great;
But, there's something more important, I think!
Those happy, little, shouts of glee...
Matt's in the lake, Alex is climbing a tree!
Little Soph just tags along...singing herself a happy song.
Jack, in his swing, just laughs and smiles...
All of them happy...for awhile!
What matters in life is not the work to be done
But little ones laughing and having such fun
And visiting Gramma, cuz anything goes!
And, I always like to tickle their toes!
We're laughing and playing and having such fun...
But still, there is all of that work to be done!
Who cares? Who cares?
We're playing today!
Let's not let ol' work get in our way!
Ten years from now, the work won't matter,
We'd rather be mixin up pancake batter!
We all had such fun...playing together,
Even though today there's stormy weather!
Cuz in our hearts the sun is out
That really makes us want to shout!
The End!

Written by Alex and Gramma
My Grandson told me what to say...
"Now, let's make it a poem, Gramma."

My Wormy Wormy Story

"Gramma, Gramma, quick, come see...
The creature that just crawled to me!
I don't dare hold him, he might bite,"
Oh, my goodness, such a fright!

"Look, I can hold him in my hand...
And he wiggles when he's in the sand,
Wormy, wormy, let's go for a walk...
But, wormy, wormy, you can't talk!
You've got no eyes, no mouth, no nose...
Or teeth inside, I don't suppose!"

I put my wormy, wormy on the ground
But he got stamped on; my brother's around!
I cried and cried, big, huge tears...
But wait, he's still alive it appears!

"Oh, wormy, wormy, you're so cute...
I just might dress you in a suit!
"Wait, you won't wiggle...
You won't crawl...
Oh well, I guess for now, that's all!
Better go find a new wormy, wormy!"

(Long ago, a wormy pet for Alex)
Not so much for Matthew, I guess ☺)

The New Group

There seems to be a group of us, babyboomers,
whose faces have taken on a new expression recently.
An expression, worn on the faces, whose depth
can only be coming straight from the heart.
Those people who have, for the most part, already reared
their own children.
Those faces, as I search the lines of wisdom (hard earned I might add)
Look not quite young...yet not quite old but somewhere in between.
They are not the faces of young, new parents,
Proud yet exhausted from lack of last night's sleep...
but older faces, proud and shining...
Maybe a tad tired from all the years of concern, prayers and care...
The recent lines softened, with a love that knows no limits, no boundaries.
These are the new Grandparents. That wonderful new group
of human beings who cannot hide their pride and affection
and fascination in the new, little lives in which
they are so blessed to share!
The reward is golden! No academy award, no standing ovation,
no pay check, (no matter how large) no promotion,
nothing else feels the same as this. Nothing in this old world!
Never before, did I know the heart could melt like a bowl of butter
in the midday sun at a glance and a smile
and chubby arms outstretched for your hug!
Never before, except at the birth of my own beautiful daughters,
did I see babies so freshly and perfectly given from Heaven itself!
Never before could coo's and patty-caked, dimpled hands
bring such tears of joy and laughter to my life!

. . .

This new breed of Grandparents, can coddle, kiss, caress
and enjoy these gifts from God freely.
Long before any syllables are uttered, you notice that look,
of happy recognition, upon those tiny faces, as they appear at your door
and embrace you with those chubby, sticky, little arms.
And, then, one day, the word comes out,
Unexpectedly, yet, long-awaited...
They gaze into your eyes and utter the precious word
THEY have chosen for only you!
"Gramma, Nanu, Mowpow, Nana, Yamma, Yampa, Boompa, Grandma,
Grandpa, MiMi, Juice, PaPa, whatever your special title has now become...
forever!
Once again, your "butter-heart" melts as you smile joyfully at this little
miracle before you!
They KNOW me! They gave me a new name!
One that will last for the remainder of your life...one that will grab your
attention no matter when or where you happen to be!

I study the faces of the new Grandma's and Grandpa's, as they hold these
little ones at stores, at church, and I now understand!

I am blessed, indeed!
I feel their pride, their joy, their rapt attention...I am one with them.
Perhaps that's why the word is GRANDchild.

For in your eyes, none are grander, or cuter or smarter.
I find that quite universal.
And, as with your own children, when that name is uttered...
it is as awesome with the 2nd, and the 3rd and the 4th
as it was with the first one! This love is GRAND!

"To be loved by ones so new, so fresh, so innocent, is likened to being
kissed by an angel! It is not a small thing when one is loved and hugged
and chosen by one so newly sent from God!"

Five Cents a Cup

I am a Gramma.
I'm 51 years old.
Today is Sunday.
After church, our grandsons came home with us.
It is September 24th.
It's cold outside.
But...
"We need to have a Kool-Aid stand...
Gramma, p-l-e-a-s-e!!!"
"Right now, Gramma!"
I am a Gramma.
I understand their plea.
So, I do what any Gramma would do.
We make Kool-Aid, we get out cups and napkins.
We get out chips.
I find a card table and a table cloth.
I even help them yell: "Kool-Aid, 5 cents a cup!"
I pay for many cups. Grampa pays for many cups.
We make more Kool-Aid because we drank it all up.
Some kind people stop. Some teen-age girls who say:
"Oh, they're so cute! I used to sell Kool-Aid!"
They pay 25 cents a cup!
A couple more girls stop. They're cute.
A grandpa and his grown-up grandson
stop and buy some.
It's getting colder out! Brrrrrrrrr
The boys mama and her friends stop by.

. . .

We are selling Kool-Aid in September on a cold day
because we believe we can! And, so we do!
(Life lesson here)
And, I, for one, will never forget
this cold day in September.
I'm 51 years old.
But, I'm in my driveway...
selling Kool-Aid to strangers
with my grandsons
because I am a Gramma!
This is not just "sugar" in our Kool-Aid,
It's the sweetness of life...
The nectar of God's blessings...
The richness of childhood's belief...
The embracing of childhood
and innocence of a child's world...
I am rich beyond belief...
At five cents a cup...
Yes, I am a Gramma!

♪ Popsicle Sticks ♪

POPSICLE STICKS ON THE KITCHEN FLOOR...
CHILDREN HOLLERIN' PLAY SOME MORE,
"Gramma, stop and see me play...
Hide and seek then run awayyyy" ♪

Popsicle sticks on the kitchen floor...
Rosy, little faces that I adore!
Filled with energy, filled with glee,
Chanting, "Gramma, look at meEEE!" ♪

Popsicle sticks on the kitchen floor...
Silly, little toys are scattered galore,
Brown-eyed girl just past me flew...
Following closely was little, "me toooo" ♪

Sister "Soso" is running too fast...
Little "me too" is always last!
Popsicle sticks on the kitchen floor...
Summer's here, who could ask for more?
Bright, little eyes that sparkle and shine,
Little feet that dance, Grandbabies are fine!
Popsicle sticks on the kitchen floor...
Children hollerin' play some more,
"Gramma, stop and see me play...
Hide and seek then run awayyyy" ♪

(A song we made up as we threw a huge bag of popsicle sticks on the floor and danced all around the kitchen)

♪ My Fishin' Song ♪

The sun is warm...the sky is blue...
I'm goin' fishy, fishy, fishin' with you.
I got my pole...got my line...
I got the feelin' we will have a great time
I'm goin' fishy, fishy, fishin' with you.

This day is perfect and you are too...
So come along with me out on the blue
Throw in a line...
I've got the bait...
I'm gonna catch "you" I can hardly wait
I'm done with my wishin'
Cuz I'm goin' fishin' "for" you!

You are my very best "catch" yet
I don't even need to get my feet wet
But I've been wishin' for such a long time
Today's the day I think I'll bring in the line...
I'm goin' fishy, fishy, fishin' for "you!"

I've got the hook, I've brought the bait...
For this catch I can hardly wait!
I'm throwin' in my sinker, hook and line...
The water ripples, ohhhhh I'm feelin' so fine

Come on along, I said the fishin's so good
Come be my buddy, well, I sure wish you would
I'm goin' fishy, fishy, fishin' "for you!"

(written for my fishin' buddy, while fishing.)

Just Do It

Laugh at the "un-laughable"...

Love the "un-loveable"...

Sing the "un-singable" song...

Right the "un-rightable" wrong...

Stop the "un-stopable"...

Play the "un-playable"...

Say the "un-sayable"...

Do the thing that "can't" be done!

From morning till the setting sun

"you" be the one to do it...

Get through it...just do it!!!

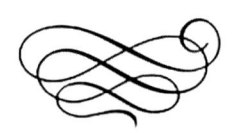

A Wonderful Wednesday Adventure

His question came out strong and clear
As we drove home from school one day;
"Gramma, do you know how to sew,
Could you make me a cape to play?"
I really want to dress all up
And look like Superman,
But, I don't have a cape to wear
A store might have one, we could stop...
I wonder if we can?

"He's really strong and really good
And he can really fly
And his red cape goes whoosh, whoosh and swirls
As he goes whirling by!"
His plea was earnest, as he spoke
My heart began to melt,
As I realized he would soon be grown;
His urgency, I felt,
To find the suit or find the cape
So he could "really fly,"
Just like a couple years ago
When he was just a little guy.

. . .

AND, SO, WE DROVE RIGHT TO THE STORE
AND WHAT DO YOU SUPPOSE?
I SAID WHAT ANY GRAMMA WOULD,
"WE NEED SUPERMAN CLOTHES!"

I GLANCED AROUND BUT NONE IN SIGHT
(I BREATHED A SILENT PRAYER)
THIS GRAMMA ASKED THE "SUPERMAN"
(AND, AS USUAL, HE WAS THERE.)
FOR IN THE BACK, UNSEEN TO US
SHE FOUND ONE, JUST HIS SIZE!...
WE PULLED IT OUT, WE HELD IT UP,
AND MUCH TO OUR SURPRISE...
**IT FIT JUST RIGHT
IT HAD A CAPE
SO HE COULD REALLY FLY**
I WISH YOU COULD HAVE SEEN THE LOOK
UPON THAT LITTLE GUY!

IT DIDN'T MATTER WHAT IT COST
FOR WE HAD FOUND OUR TREASURE,
AND THE JOY UPON THAT LITTLE FACE,
WAS WORTH MORE THAN GOLD COULD MEASURE!

• • •

His older brother got gold coins
One hundred forty four,
And a ball that bounced real crazy...
Said, he needed nothing more!
But we found some goo
That glowed in green
He thought that might be fun...
We filled our cart with silly stuff
Then decided we were done.
It wasn't just the "stuff" we bought
Though that had been our goal...
But the memories we created,
That was sacred in our soul.
These memories that would never fade,
The bonds so close, so dear...
A Gramma and her GRANDsons
And our Jesus, always near!

(Matthew was 8 and Alex was 9 years old)
(Matthew was Superman)

A Wonderful Wednesday

Wednesday's are wonderful and I'll tell you why,
I pick up our boys and the time seems to fly!
I drive to their school at a quarter past two
And I smile as I wait
For their class to march through.
For they must raise their hands
To be excused from the line
And before they turn the corner of the school,
Their eyes meet mine!
Their hands fly, high,
Eyes fixed on me...
Their waving hands held high, I see!
Who's most excited, them or me?
To be together, to be turned free...
The hugs, the grins, the special glance,
And, in the parking lot, we dance!
Now, in the convertible we laugh and talk nonstop
We munch on treats...
Forget the clock!
There's tales to tell about the day
And jokes to laugh at
And tricks to play!

• • •

We fly on home and rarely stop,
Unless they pick a special spot...
For we have so much to say and do
Our hearts are happy
Thru and thru!
For, it's "Wonderful Wednesday,"
That's what they say...
When they wake up in their beds that day,
Their MaMa smiles and says, "that's true,"
Gramma & Grampa will be there for you,
And then you can go home and play,
And share special times
For today's Wednesday!

Little One

Your questions are endless,
Oh, Little One, Little One...
Close your eyes now and rest,
Oh, Little One, Little One...
Your world is so simple, so clean and so right,
I embrace you, my Little One,
Goodnight Now, Goodnight!
Life is an adventure, exciting and fun,
You are an example, to me, Little One.
The flowers and leaves bring your
sigh of surprise,
And, wonder and joy fill those big,
trusting eyes!
With an "Ohhh" and an "Ahhh" and a
"Quick come and see"...
You re-open the treasures Life offers to me!
For a bug or a fish bring you hours of fun
And, to hurry...for what?
Little One, Little One.
If we would take notice, if we could just see
And, remember the joy at age 2 or age 3...
And, for ONE DAY, take the time
To reflect and to rest;
To "Re-spond" to life's beauty
Without feeling stressed!

. . .

Take the hand of a child,
By a wee-one be led
For an up-lifting spirit,
And your heart will be fed.
You will feel all the sparkle
Come back to your eyes,
And, may let our a whisper,
To your own surprise!
Your world, for one moment,
Becomes simple and right...
We can learn from you,
Little One...
Good Night, Oh, Good Night!

Love you, Alex!
Gramma
xo

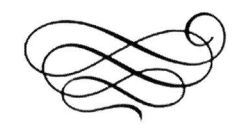

Gabo, Bompa, Please Come See

Gabo, Bompa, please come see
The video that's on TV
Hug-A-Bug, my favorite show...
My brother and cousins all love it so.
We cuddle up, so warm and cozy...
Matt and Jack, Alex and Sosie.
We have such fun, we giggle, we play
We beg our parents,
"p-l-e-a-s-e- c-a-n-w-e s-t-a-y"?
With my big-boy cousins I love to play
And so, when Patrick takes my boys away...
I stand at Gabo's door and yell real loud,
"I want my boys back home, here, NAWWW!"

All by myself, I climb the stairs
"I'm at the top, whoo hooo, No cares!"
"All by myself," right down the slide
It's really fun, I love the ride!

Next, we run down to the lake,
Of course, our "fishy poles" we take,
"I want to be out on the dock...
So, holding Mommy's hand, we walk,
Far, far out there...by the water...
A little "Fisher-Daddy's Daughter!"

• • •

I am two years old
We run forth and back...
Next-year I'll run along with Jack!
But for now, he watches and laughs as we play,
It won't be long; he'll be crawling our way!

So, "Gabo, Bompa, quick, come see!
We're playing, playing, running free!
Tonight we'll close our eyes real tight,
And dream adventures left and right,
Then sleep and rest the night away...
Tomorrow's another day to play!"

(Love you, Sophie)

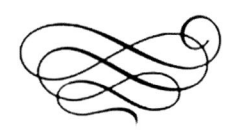

Treasures

A precious little flower is tucked gently in my hand…
It goes inside our "treasure box,"
That's its place, "we understand."
Sometimes no words are spoken…
As he opens up my hand,
And places in it a rock, a feather,
Or a bobber from the sand.
But we both know, without a word,
The meaning of his treasure;
The look shines deeply from those eyes
With love I cannot measure!
And sometimes, when we're all alone
We open up the box…
Making sure they've all been placed,
The fish bones, weeds and rocks.
And, one by one, we put them back;
Arranging them, "just so,"
Takes time and must be done "just right,"
You have to go real "s-l-o-w.
This ritual between us has a meaning rich and strong…
For these treasures, given lovingly,
Will remain, our whole lives long.

. . .

A stick, a twig, an acorn...

A penny and a string...

Are simple little gifts

But such happiness they bring!

They may as well be sunshine,

Or contentment...with a bow;

Or peacefulness, in shiny wrap,

Or a laugh, for when you're low.

They may as well be solid gold...

Or a diamond, rich and rare...

For the joy runs deep within the heart

That always wants to share!

Yes, the treasure's here,

Before our eyes,

In these precious little ones;

Our God has richly blessed us

With grand daughter and grand sons!

(Written for Alexander long ago)

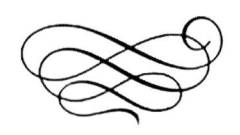

SOSO

YOU HAVE STOLEN OUR HEARTS
LITTLE BROWN EYED GIRL...
WITH YOUR SENSE OF WONDER
AT ALL THE NEW WORLD.
YOUR GIGGLES AND LAUGHS
AND WONDERFUL SMILE
SIMPLY MELT OUR HEARTS
AND MAKES DAYS WORTHWHILE!
YOUR BABY FEET TODDLE
AS YOU BABBLE AND COO
AND WHISPER, "HIDE, HIDE"
AS YOU PLAY PEEK-A-BOO!
YOU ARE HIDING YOUR FACE
AND YOU THINK WE CAN'T SEE
UNTIL YOU PEEK OUT AT US
THEN GIGGLE WITH GLEE.
WE HUG AND WE DANCE,
AND THE WHOLE WORLD IS NEW
TO THOSE BIG BROWN EYES
THAT YOU'RE LOOKING THRU!
THE OH'S AND THE AHHH'S
AND JUST SHEER DELIGHT
RE-AWAKEN OUR HEARTS
MAKING EVERYTHING RIGHT!
OUR SWEET LITTLE SOPHIE,
A BLESSING SO TRUE...
HERE'S A HUG AND A KISS
MA'AM AND BOMPA LOVE YOU!
XO

This Five Year Old Boy

Our little Jack, with big, brown eyes
is quick to laugh and show surprise.
His Christmas request was clear & strong...
A "pink rose or red one"...
to last all year long.

He loves a flower or butterfly
appreciates colors in the sky.
He'll "stop" anytime
that there's beauty to see
and he always makes sure
that he shares it with me!

Our little Jack, our pride and joy
our handsome little Grandson boy!
He's quick to help and filled with cheer.
It makes you want to keep him near!
The world's wonders are his toy
so ready for fun, this five year old boy!

BROTHER, FRIEND & BUDDY

MY BROTHER AND I HAVE SO MUCH FUN
WE RUN AND PLAY IN THE SUMMER SUN!
WE LAUGH AND JUMP INTO THE LAKE
AND IN THE SAND OUR PIES WE BAKE.
WE SWIM, LIKE FISH AND KICK OUR FEET;
YES, LIVING ON THE LAKE IS NEAT!
WHEN MOM SAYS, "YES, RUN THRU THE HOSE,"
WE GO REAL FAST AND PLUG OUR NOSE!
IT'S SLIPPERY AND WE SOMETIMES FALL...
OH, WATER FUN IS SUCH A BALL!
YES, HE'S MY BROTHER, FRIEND AND BUDDY
AND IN OUR WAGON WE ACT SO NUTTY!
WE TAKE A BATH, WE DO THE DISHES,
BUT OUR FAVORITE THING IS CATCHING FISHES!
WE KEEP OUR MOTHER AWFULLY BUSY...
AT TIMES SHE SAYS WE MAKE HER DIZZZZZY!
WE'RE JUST LIKE TWINS, SOME PEOPLE SAY,
WE'RE "DOUBLE-TROUBLE" THRU THE DAY!
BUT THEN, WE'RE ALSO "DOUBLE FUN,"
WHEN WE DRESS ALIKE
YOU CAN'T TELL WHICH ONE!
YES, HE'S BY BUDDY, BROTHER, FRIEND,
AND SO, FOR NOW, THIS IS THE END!

(Dedicated to Alex & Matthew)

BEHOLD THE CHILD AT PLAY

THESE BOYS, MY JOYS,
MAKE LIFE COMPLETE.
THEIR ANTICS AMUSE
AND ARE PLEASANTLY SWEET!
THEY FILL ME AND FREE ME
AND MAKE MY HEART SING;
AS I ABANDON ADULTHOOD
MY "CHILD" TAKES WING!

THEY MAKE LIFE A TREASURE,
A THRILL TO BE LIVED...
AND SAVORED AND FLAVORED,
THEIR "ALL" DO THEY GIVE!
SO RUN ALONG AND TASTE THE WIND
AS IT RUSTLES THROUGH YOUR HAIR
AND PLAY OUTSIDE UNTIL IT'S DARK
I WONDER, DO YOU DARE?

YOU'RE SURE TO TASTE THE SWEETNESS
AND THE WONDER YOU'LL RECEIVE
IF YOU WANDER WITH A CHILD...
YOU WILL FIND SUCH A GREAT REPRIEVE!
YOUR HEART WILL SING
YOU'LL DANCE WITH GRACE
A WINNING SMILE UPON YOUR FACE
EMBRACING LIFE ALONG THE WAY...
BEHOLD...
THE CHILD, NOW AT PLAY!

(The joy of being their "Gramma" waiting to give Alex & Matthew a ride home from school and watching them play on the playground...)

Today's Reality

I opened up a Snapchat...
His laughter filled my heart,
Although his face I could not see
For we now live far apart.

I played it over and over...
Just listening to his sound,
I felt a twinge within my heart
Since now he's not around.

Then I clicked on Instagram...
Her face appeared in a flash,
My, how she's getting older
As these couple years flew past!

I treasure fleeting instances...
When I might see or hear,
My grandchildren, so far away
Whom I hold, Oh, so dear!

My heart, it seems, just fills with glee...
When randomly I chance to see,
A glimpse, a glance,
For a moment or two
Our Texas family, we love you!

"Blue Rose"
Original watercolor painting by Jack Henry Nguyen

Here's Me…Just Sayin'…

Our "smart phones" indeed are very smart!
Computers, tablets, watches, smart phones
have become our cherished "pets!"
They have actually taken the place of them in our lives.
We hold them close and coddle them!
We exercise them daily, feeding them with chargers
at night or when they are "low."
We even give them "treats" shiny, sparkly new cases…
and lots of "apps" to feed them and watch them grow.
Some of us act as if we lost a best friend when they die…
as if nothing could ever replace them.
We take them on vacations with us, asking, in advance,
making sure that the place has wifi or coverage
for our "precious pets"
They've become an actual "appendage"
attached to our bodies, almost closer than our skin ☺
They hold countless photos of all occasions of our lives!
Also of all the people we know and love!
Some hold all of our most personal information.
The very second a thought crosses our mind
it goes on facebook or twitter or instagram or snapchat
or one of many many other sights.
Pictures of every meal we eat out is shared with all of our "friends"
instantly before we consume it!

• • •

The babies born are instantly seen ☺
the ones we love who die are instantly shared...
our occasions are on the media almost before they happen.
When you reach out your hand, chances are you'll be reaching out to
grasp someone's smart phone in their hand.
They have replaced old fashioned phone calls.
Instead of actually hearing another human voice,
we text one another. Very convenient.
(Let your fingers do the talking.)
There is no need to travel. They connect us to the entire world,
instantly. To see a new site,
I never dreamed I'd be saying, "google it up,"
Or text me a picture or send out an "Evite" to my gathering.
And, why read the obituaries in the "newspaper" of all things!!!
Open your facebook and find out which person died last night.
So be certain to grab your coffee cup or Mountain Dew
"before" you open your facebook or your text.....
you never know what you will find!!!
How smart are they really? Well,
They take our time, our hard-earned money, our caresses,
they are very smart indeed, I'd say.
They are best friends and our entertainment.
Spelling, punctuation, handwriting, snail mail, obsolete!!!
Abbreviate everything.

• • •

We can "friend" everyone and if you disagree with them in any way,
just "unfriend" them....no need to visit.
Our heads are bent down as we walk past another human being
who may be smiling at us or saying hello
(tho many times, at the grocery store, I've said hello
to someone whom I think is saying hello to me but
I don't see their earbuds haha lol !!!!
They excuse me because they see how old I am ☺)
They could have a tear in their eye, or seek a warm hello
from a real, live person.
Bluetooth does not mean needing a dental implant ......
Snapchat does not mean "chating using your mouth,"
Google it up is not feeling sick ☺ blahh.
There are hundreds of other terms but for me,
my children and grandchildren teach me as I go along....
too much is too much for an old woman ☺
But I am glad to be experiencing it all in today's world!!!
These smart phones are both a blessing and a curse!
A blessing because it's amazing information "now."
A friend, "now." Immediate communication!
A curse, because we perhaps could be on the brink
of human extinction?
Ignoring the live, real flesh and blood individual next to us.

• • •

Soon no one will be able to spell on their own,
or use cursive handwriting on real paper with a real pen or pencil…
(or even care that they can't ☺)
or hear a human voice, (or care that they won't)
listen to YouTube instead.
Smart phones can't hug us, even tho they feel warm from use.
You don't see many children playing outside anymore…
climbing trees or playing in the park…the parks are pretty empty.
They're inside….gaming or on computers….
along with their parents who are on computers.
Our smart phones will have taken possession of us, completely.
All in all, we must not forget to use our brains, and our hearts
and our souls, Because that's something our phones
will never have, folks. Thank God!

Excuse me now, I have to run…
my cell phone is blinking ☺

"Cardinal"
Original oil painting by Dianne Goetten Krause

CHAPTER SEVEN
Friendship and Care for One Another

Being Kind

Oh, I didn't know, I just didn't see…
That day you passed me, silently.
Your burdens were heavy…
Your spirit was low…
You were weak and afraid…
If I only could know.
If only I could have…and shared my smile…
Might your burdens have lifted
If, for only a while?
For we never know "How"
And we never know "Why"
But maybe we shouldn't just
"Pass-right-on-By"
When maybe, your smile,
could heal someone's heart…
And you may never know
But that was "your" part!
So, let us all try to lighten the way
And, ease someone's burdens
As we go thru our day…
For the "weary-of-heart,"
Let's all do our part
Maybe ease other's minds,
If, by just "being kind."

Hearts that Listen

Friends make
Stars brighter...
Darkness lighter...
Success sweeter...
Jokes neater...
Sunshine glisten...
Hearts that listen.

They laugh with and tease...
Encourage and please...
They hold "secrets dear,"
And help "pray away" fear.

They give hugs you can count on
When you need a lift...
A friend's love is precious...
It's God's greatest gift!

Finally, all of you, be like-minded,
Be sympathetic, love one another,
Be compassionate and humble.
1 Peter 3:8

Just Stay Near

She called me crying...with barely a breath,
"It came back bad, I'm scared to death."
The terror grips a woman's being
For who knows "what" they're really seeing?
That's when she needs someone to share...
A hand to grasp...a silent prayer...
Her breath comes out in rapid gasps,
Will it be ok or bad news, perhaps?
I go...I understand her fear,
I bring my strength, I just stay near.

For just one moment, time stands still...
For my Dear Friend, I know it will.
Her future is unknown, it's true,
But our Best Friend will see her through!
Our God, our Friend, with love to spare
Will strengthen and comfort, He is there!
Listen, listen, softly still...
He hears our plea...and always will!

Come now my Friend, hold close my hand,
For, in HIS will, our lives are planned!
Dear God, be with her now, this day...
Give onto her, your strength, I pray!
Be thou her guide...help her be brave,
Resting in YOU, her life you'll save!
My Friend, have faith, be brave, walk on
Rely on God's strength and carry on!

Two are better than one...
If either of them falls down, one can help the other up.
Ecclesiastes 4:9-10

PRIDE

Somewhere along life's pathway
We're told to hide what we feel inside
So we grow up thinking that's what's right,
Don't forget, we have our pride!

The "macho man," the "women's lib,"
The teen-age, "I don't care,"
The attitudes of, "I am strength,"
Are getting us nowhere.

For one alone is awfully weak
No matter what our masks proclaim
We need each other's weaknesses,
For thru that, our strength we'll gain.

To admit we're weak
Will make us strong,
And maybe help us see...
As we peel off our needless masks,
"I'm amazed, he's just like me!"

Refugees...Who Cares?

Refugee...a foreign world
A homeless people drift at sea...
Hungry stomachs, pain and death...
But far removed from you and me.

To us, they're nameless faces,
The news tells us of their plight...
But we have food and blankets warm,
We will lose no sleep tonight!

Does our country have enough right now?
Jobs to find and mouths to feed...
Have we become so very wealthy...
That we can't relate to need?

And what if WE were one of them,
And heard OUR child cry...
But could only sit in agony...
While WE watched a loved one die?

Just think a moment, how YOU'D feel,
If YOUR children were not fed...
And you had no place you could call home...
Just tomorrows filled with dread.

Refugee...If I were one,
My prayer, to God, would be...
For "Someone" out there, just like YOU...
To take me in and set me free!

• • •

This poem was written in 1979 …
It came to pass, many years later,
the man who became our son-in-law had come to our Country
on a boat back then…..a refugee.

*Have mercy on me, my God, have mercy on me,
for in You I take refuge. I will take refuge in the
shadow of Your wings until the disaster has passed.
Psalm 57:1*

Kindness Seeds

The goodness and mercy that our God sends
Is often displayed in the warm heart of friends!
It is shown to us daily, in words and in deeds...
And the kindness is scattered and spread by those seeds.

Those people who give,
with no thought of what's owed...
Knowing burdens are heavy...
They lighten our load.

For, their goodness shines forth...
As a beacon of light,
And gives honor and glory to God, in His might!

For the prayer that was uttered in silence, alone...
Has been answered, most deeply,
By the love that's been shown!

Let us ever remember to thank Him, in prayer...
For His steadfast, safe keeping, that is constantly there!

Can You See Me?

Do you see the need beneath that face?
A need held deep within…
Do you hear a silent pleading,
Underneath that happy grin?

Buried deep beneath that confidence,
Or the hassled, hurried way…
Can you catch a glimpse of the lonely man
Who could use your love today?

Have you ever stopped to think
No matter what your "lot" may be…
We all need another's loving touch,
I need you and you need me.

But we're adults, we're all grown up,
It's such a risk to say…
"Hey friend, I really need a hug,
I'm low on love today."

So, most of us just march right on,
With our secure and happy smile…
When what we'd really like to say,
Is, "Talk with me awhile."

"Love me, need me, be my friend,
Let me share my life with you…"
How shocked we'd be,
If we only knew…
How many need us too!

Remember

She thinks differently than I do,
Her views are not like mine...
I think maybe I'll avoid her...
As far as I'm concerned, that's fine!

He has a funny attitude,
He comes across too strong...
Why try to understand this guy...
It would take a whole life long!

I expected her to love me,
In a "certain kind of way"
She didn't love the way she should...
She's not worth my time of day!

Isn't this the way we feel,
A lot of times in life...
When thoughts don't coincide with ours...
And others cause us strife?

Self-righteousness can sneak right in,
It's "our way" ... that is all!
We cannot see the other's view...
Which makes us very small.

We are called to love each other,
Not to turn and walk away...
From a person who is different...
Might we love him if we stay?

• • •

If we try to see inside her,
Who she is and where she's been...
And if we ask God to help us love...
Could this person be a friend?

Perhaps we shouldn't judge so fast,
Our decision could be wrong...
Remember...they rejected One...
Who was, " Jesus," ... all along!

Lord, give me eyes that I may see,
Lest I, as people will, should pass by
Someone's Calvary...and think it's just a hill.
Author unknown

Pass It On

It's good to know there's someone strong
On whom I can depend...
A loving shoulder to lean upon
When troubles have no end.
And kind, warm eyes that look at me
And say, "I understand,"
And tears that fall, along with mine,
A warm and tender hand...
That reaches out in times of need
And times of happiness too...
And joyous smiles and silly laughs,
That share your jokes with you.
For, in my life, I've been so blessed
With the people that surround me,
That the love they give and the lives they live,
Won't cease but to astound me.

Any good that's in me or any good I may share
With another, is only possible...
Because of the ones who care.
Who care and give their love to me,
And share their thoughts and dreams,
Who radiate their strength in me
Recharging mine, it seems.
They give me strength to love, to live,
To be the best I can,
To take one small step forward
For the betterment of man.

• • •

I've been so blessed with loving people
That I sometimes forget to see…
That there are those who have no one,
Less fortunate than me.
Why God blessed me with so many
In my life, I'll never know…
But I'm thankful and I'll take their love
And try to let it show.
I'll try to pass it on to those I meet from day to day
And they, in turn, will pass it on
To those who come their way.
And if we all keep sharing love,
And strength with those we meet…
There will be none left
Who have no one,
And give up in defeat.
Because they'll have their someone strong,
On whom they can depend…
A loving shoulder to lean upon,
When troubles have no end!

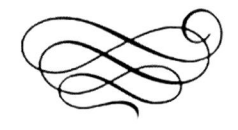

Butterflies and Broken Wings

"All my butterflies are broken, Mom,
All their wings are crushed and torn,
And I'll never find some other ones..."
She sobbed and looked forlorn.

Her world was torn to pieces
In her butterflies broken wings...
She had worked so hard to catch them all,
They were her priceless things.

Now, she, herself, my butterfly,
Has a torn and broken wing...
Now I'm the one to cry and pray,
That her heart again, will sing.

I pray to God, to find a way
To help this one that's torn...
But the days and nights are awfully long
And I feel so very worn.

My butterfly is broken
And my world is torn apart,
And we must patch her broken wings...
And calm her tender heart.

By we, I mean the Lord and me...
Our butterfly must mend,
Before her wings are crushed too much...
And there is no help to send.

A day will come, and soon, I know,
When she'll be soaring high...
And our tears will turn to smiles then,
My butterfly and I.

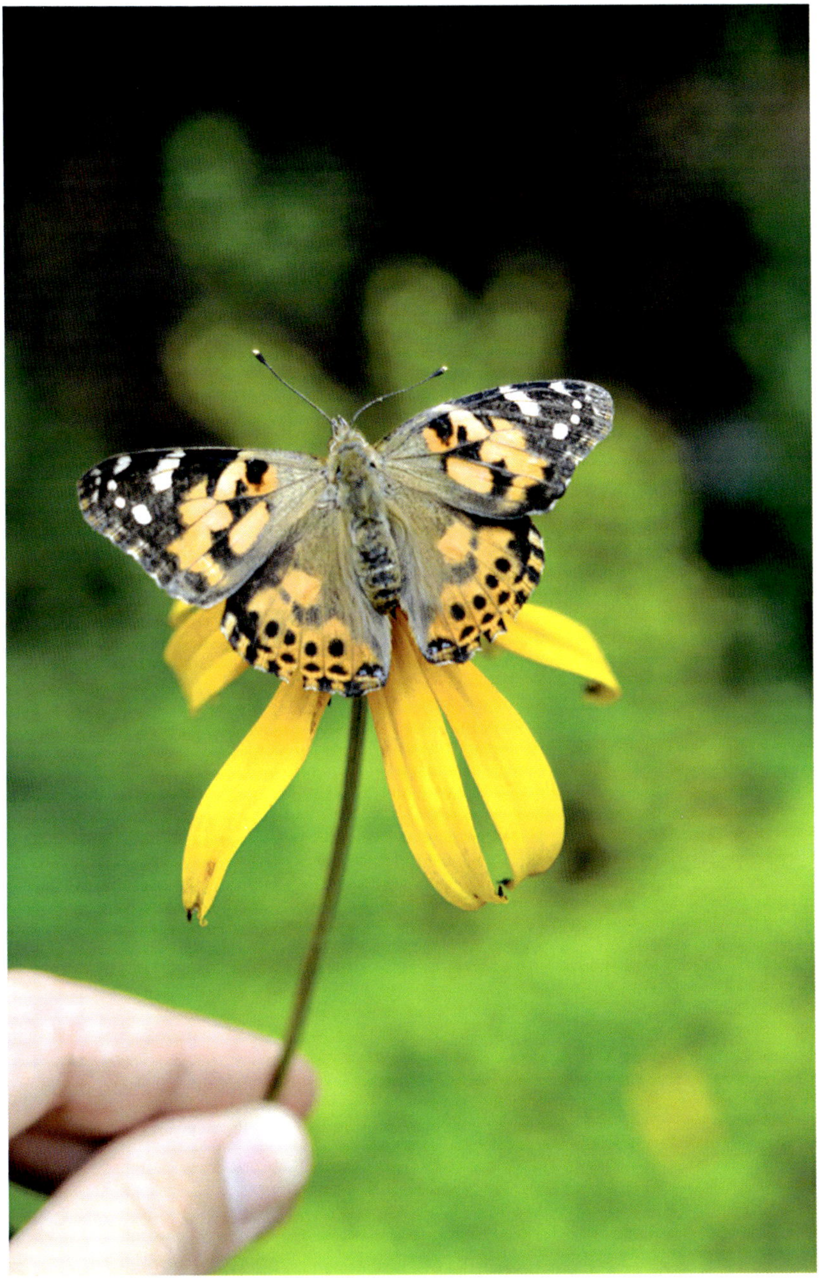

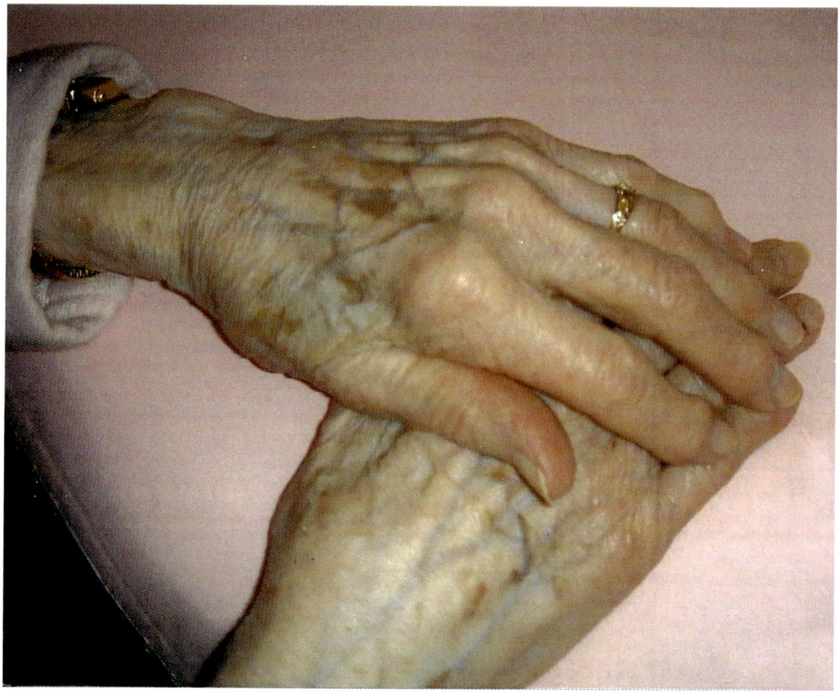

CHAPTER EIGHT
Memories of Mother and Aging

When I Grow Old

If I grow old and forget your name
and my memory fades away...
I know your heart will hurt inside
Then that's the time to pray.
Our "dress rehearsal" does not last...
Our life on earth will soon be past!
We will walk on, to another place
Where we'll see Jesus, face to face.
Imagine how thrilling it will be
When Jesus stands with you, with me!
This life is but a fleeting glance....
A momentary circumstance,
Which God has given for a while...
While he walks, with us, thru each trial.
Embrace this life, and do your best
Allowing God to do the rest,
For difficulties never last....
So hold on tight...they'll soon be past.
Stand up...walk on...be brave...be true,
for Jesus always cares for you!
His hand is always open wide,
Hold on....hold on...His love abides!

Reflection...
I was thinking of my Mother, at the end, when she forgot who I was
she looked up at me and said, "Can I ask you something?"
I said, "of course," she smiled and sweetly
and softly asked, "who are you?"

I will never forget you, see, I have engraved you
on the palms of my hands.
Isaiah 49:16

Mom's Poem

I looked out of my window just this morning,
The apple blossoms were so pretty there.
The birds and all the little, wild creatures,
Were enjoying all the crumbs
That I tossed out to share.

I looked up to the sky, into the forever;
And thanked my Friend that's living there,
For each and every one of my seven Children,
Each one of them so fair!

Each day I want to shout it to the hill tops,
Thanks for borrowing each one of them to me;
My Daughters are like a lovely garden,
And my son is the greatest Son, you see!

And when I reach the home of my Redeemer,
I'll look into His eyes and say,
"Please save a space in this beautiful place,
For my Children, my Husband and Me!"

After my Mother died, in 2008,
I found this poem...
Written By: Helene Bergh Goetten

Thank you, Mom!

Age

I can see your eyes have now grown dim…
You falter, as you walk…
Your tears are quick to surface
As I sit with you and talk.

For you realize, far more than I,
In my youth, I couldn't know…
My words come fast and easily
While your speech is soft and slow.

For you now have wisdom, with your years
And, I am slow to see…
That you have pain…
what's hard for you, comes easily to me.

I move so quickly, life's pace is fast
There's so much to be done…
While you move slowly, perhaps you know
Life's race is almost run!

Perhaps you see what youth cannot
The treasure life can hold…
We will learn much, if we s-l-o-w down,
Learn much, from one who's old!

There will be pain if we touch their hearts
If we "really" pause to see…
That growing old is lonely
And, someday, it will be me!

So touch them, love them, cry a bit,
Experience their pain…
And you will find, as ne'er before…
Great peace and strength you'll gain!

Even to your old age and grey hairs I am he, I am He who will sustain you. I have made you and I will carry you.
Isaiah 46:4

Our Treasure

She fed me and clothed me and taught me to pray…
She held my hand tightly when my skies turned to gray.
She stood, like a soldier, so steadfast and strong…
Protecting me, guiding me, all my life long!
She cheered up my days with her smile and her song…
Her whistle, her wisdom was:
"Laugh and be strong!"

She made pianos come to life, as she easily caressed
Those "black keys," which poured forth a strain
That was better than the best!

She was the true epitome
Of, "use the gifts God gave to me,
Use them well and share them too,
Be thankful for where God plants you!"

So, hum a tune or tell a story
Whistle, loudly, for God's glory!
Sing a song out…loud and clear
For all the world to lend an ear.
For when we do…we give her honor
We breathe our blessings all upon her!
Her memory will live, forever
Her life will always be our treasure!

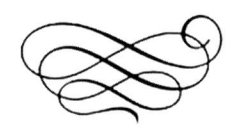

My MaMa

You asked for no words of "flowery praise,"
Then how could I tell
How you blessed all our days?
How your kindness shone through, every trial
We knew...as we grew.

Your music, your laughter, stays here, Ever-after...
My heart is aglow with the love you did show,
Day after day, in your unselfish way.

By your gentle care, we became quite aware
Of God's love for us all...the big and the small.
You taught us to care, to love and to give,
These lessons I'll treasure, as long as I live!

My MaMa, my Friend, your life will not end.
But go on in our smiles,
Our laughs and our dreams!
My Mom is an angel...in my world it seems!

I love you, forever, Mom, your Daughter

Gayle

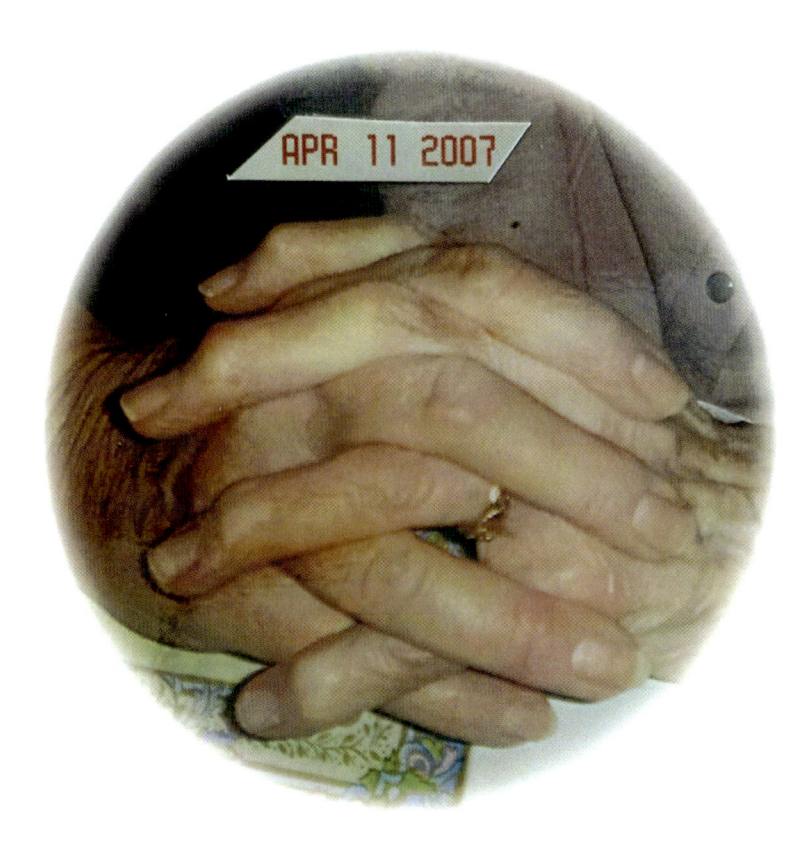

*This is a photo of her hand in mine...
Taken one year to the day
before she died...*

Memories While Shopping

I passed by the candies and jars of cashews,
And then, very slowly, the "Keds" tennis shoes.
Then, "Alfred Dunner," the outfits were fine,
Oh, my heart is missing that sweet Mom of mine!

I see the white blouses with "Peter-Pan" collars,
And my thoughts go to her,
Passing out silver dollars!
Her treasures to us at Christmas time...
Her memory lives in this heart of mine!

The carols play out loud and clear,
They're not the same, no, not this year!
Instead of joy and Christmas cheer
I wipe away a lonely tear...
And try to celebrate the season
But I feel quite sad, I have a reason.
The lights don't sparkle, the bulbs don't shine
I miss, I miss, that Mom of mine!

Although I know she had to leave us
To bake a cake for Baby Jesus!

• • •

She lights the candles and sings her song,
"Happy Birthday, Dear Jesus"
Her voice now strong!
Her smile, her laughter, resounds 'cross the sky...
While over the "black keys" her fingers now fly
"Be happy, it's Christmas!" my Mother would say...
While she makes angels happy
In her own special way.
So, Christmas it is, I shall celebrate too...
Cuz it's my way of saying, "Oh, Mom, I love you!"

Merry Christmas, Mom!

I was 59 years old...this was my first Christmas Eve without her!

"Birthday Cake"
Original oil painting by Dianne Goetten Krause

OUR DRESS REHEARSAL

IF I COULD JUST TALK TO YOU ONE MORE TIME…
IF ONLY MY PHONE RANG, WITH YOU ON THE LINE.
IF ONLY I HEARD YOUR WONDERFUL LAUGHTER,
IT WOULD ECHO AND RING IN MY HEART, EVER- AFTER.
IF WE COULD JUST VISIT AND TALK FOR AWHILE,
ONCE MORE, I THINK, THEN, I COULD SMILE.
FOR, MORNING AND EVENING AND AFTERNOON TOO,
I MISS YOU, I MISS YOU, MOM, TRULY I DO!
ALL OF THE YEARS THAT I HAD YOU HERE…
COULD NEVER BE ENOUGH, I FEAR!
ONE MORE CALL, ONE MORE TALK, ONE MORE LAUGH,
ONE MORE WALK, ONE MORE SMILE, JUST FOR AWHILE…
THIS HOLLOW SPACE WITHIN MY HEART
IT WILL, FOREVER, BE A PART…
OF HOW I FEEL, DOES IT EVER HEAL?
OR JUST REMAIN AND STAY THE SAME,
WITH ALL THIS PAIN?
I TRY AND TRY TO LET YOU GO,
GUESS I DON'T REALLY WANT TO… SO,
WITHIN MY HEART, YOU WILL REMAIN
BEAUTIFUL, YOUNG AND ALWAYS THE SAME!
MY MOTHER, MY FRIEND, MY CONFIDANT TOO…
I'M PRAYING YOU KNOW JUST HOW MUCH I LOVED YOU.
THEN AND NOW AND FOREVER MORE …
MY BEAUTIFUL MOTHER, WHOM I JUST ADORE!
IN MY HEART'S MEMORY, YOUR LIFE WAS A SONG,
AND, I'LL SING IT FOREVER, FOR ALL MY LIFE LONG.

• • •

STAY CLOSE BESIDE ME THAT I CAN FEEL...
YOUR PRESENCE, STRONG AND VERY REAL.
STAY CLOSE THAT I MAY FEEL YOUR GRACE,
AND ALWAYS, ALWAYS SEE YOUR FACE!
I TREASURE EVERY MEMORY THAT LIVES WITHIN MY HEART...
AND THANK MY GOD THAT ALL MY LIFE,
YOU WILL FOREVER, BE A PART!
JUST ONE MORE TIME, JUST ONE MORE CALL,
TO HAVE YOU BACK, I'D TRADE IT ALL...

TOO SOON, TOO SOON, OUR LIVES ARE DONE,
OUR "DRESS REHEARSAL" HAS BEEN RUN!
TOO SOON, TOO SOON, OUR DAYS ARE SPENT,
AND ALL THAT'S LEFT IS OUR "INTENT."
WE TRAVEL ON TO AN UN-KNOWN LAND,
TO GRASP OUR HEAVENLY FATHER'S HAND
WE WALK AWAY FROM EVERY CARE,
AND EVERY WORRY, UNAWARE...
FOR NOW WE SEE, THE MATTER'S CLEAR,
OUR LORD, OUR SAVIOR, OH, SO NEAR!
OUR "DRESS- REHEARSAL" HAS BEEN RUN,
AND ALL TOO SOON, OUR LIVES ARE DONE.
THIS WORLD IS BUT OUR STEPPING STONE,
TO ENDLESS WORSHIP AT HIS THRONE!
FOR, WE ARE HIS AND HIS ALONE!

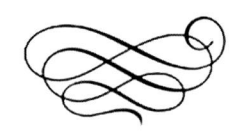

The Eternal Song

The music that you played upon the keys
when you were here~~~
Is locked, within my heart, forever more
My Mother Dear~~~
Those melodies play on and linger
In my brain~~~
And, "photo-shots" of seeing you play~~~
Within my mind, remain!
Those "twinkling" eyes of blue~~~
That looked content as fingers flew
Across those keys,
Black, if you please~~~
As you composed another song~~~
So happily, I sang along!
I can see you now, so clearly~~~
Only in my memory~~~
I can see you smiling, as you play~~~
The music flowing free!
And so, this is your legacy~~~
I hold it as my treasure~~~
My Precious Mom, My constant Friend,
I love you~~~beyond measure!

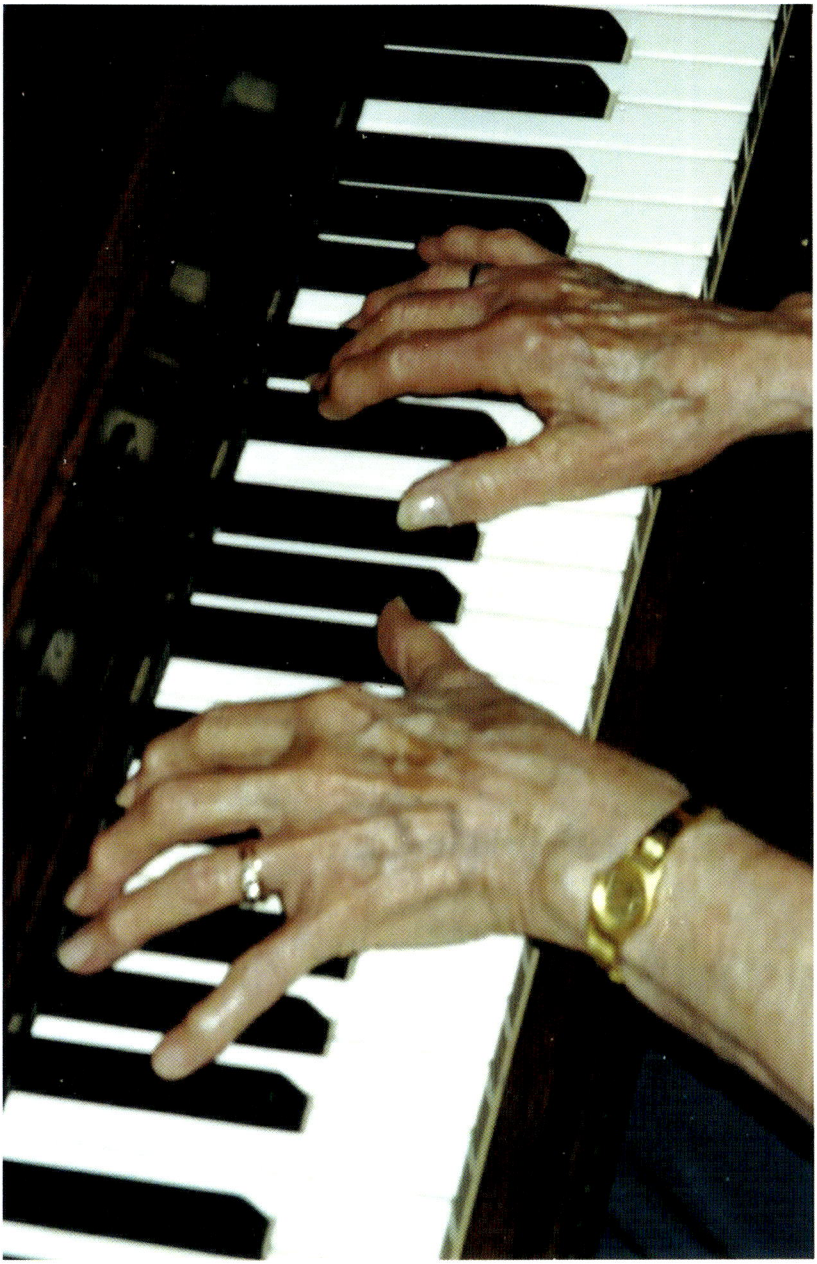

My Mother's Hands

My Mother's hands were velvet hands
Filled with such love and care...
So beautiful and tender
Thru all those years of wear.
So soft, so strong, so giving,
To all within her reach...
Her fingers gently showing
All the lessons she must teach.
Guiding and directing her family
As we grew...
Her constant presence and patient heart
Thru-out our lives, we knew.
A friend, who welcomed
All who came...
Animals, adults, babies,
All the same!

. . .

She gave "special honor,"
To all who sat...
In her kitchen for coffee
Or just a "chat."
She served and listened
And served some more...
You knew you were welcome,
At Mother's door!
So blessed, by God,
Beyond compare...
With thankfulness, I breathe this prayer,
Oh God, your blessing from above...
Most richly, touched our world
With love!

Absence

If I could call Mom on the phone,
Here's what I would have said;
"My favorite swing out on the willow… is being cut down,
the branch is dead."
I've had a swing since I was small,
And two strong men who built them all…
For me to swing and laugh and fly,
Upon the wings of air and sky.
To swing, to soar, above the earth,
To sing and swing, for all I'm worth.
Oh how I've loved to swing and fly
Inventing stories into the sky!
And Mother would have listened and smiled
With knowing eyes that said, "I understand,
My Daughter, oh, it's too bad it must come down,
I had to do that too…
The chains got weak, Dad's wooden seats and swings
Had to be through.
But through all those years I've gained so much
That thrill just never lost its touch,
A time to totally unwind
and explore recesses in my mind,
My swing, my Mom, my youth they're gone
But not the chance to sing…I still can sing my sweetest song
and so I'll sing and whistle too
And gaze into the sky…
And while I do I'll understand… my Mother didn't die;
Not in my soul or mind or heart
Forever in my world a part
Of who I am
Of what I do…for she lives on…oh Mother, I love you!

HANDS

ONE NIGHT, AMID THE GAIETY AND CONFUSION AND CHATTERING VOICES
OF A BIRTHDAY PARTY; AS WE STOOD VISITING,
MY MOTHER AND I, SHE GAVE ME A PRECIOUS GIFT, A TREASURE TO HOLD
CLOSE TO MY HEART FOR THE REST OF MY DAYS.
SHE LOOKED INTO MY EYES AND SAID SOFTLY AND CLOSELY,
"YOU KNOW, YOU ARE THE ONLY ONE OUT OF ALL THE KIDS
WHO DOES THAT... AND HOW GOOD IT FEELS AFTER ALL THESE YEARS!"
SHE WAS REFERRING TO THE FACT THAT I WAS STANDING CLOSE, HOLDING...
NO, ACTUALLY STROKING HER WONDERFULLY SOFT AND VELVETY HANDS.
I REALIZED THAT IT WAS TRUE...WHEN I WAS WITH HER I DID REACH OUT
AND CARESS HER HANDS.
IT IS OVERWHELMING TO ME TO SAVOR HER STATEMENT.
TO HOLD IT CLOSE AND REALIZE HOW VERY SIGNIFICANT
IT IS TO BE SINGLED OUT OF SEVEN, TO HAVE A SPECIAL PLACE. MOST OF
ALL, AND BEYOND WORDS, TO HAVE MY MOTHER THERE... AT THAT MOMENT,
TO HAVE THE PRIVILEGE OF HOLDING THE HANDS OF AN ANGEL. HANDS
SOFTER THAN VELVET TO THE TOUCH, HANDS AS GENTLE AS A BABY'S SKIN...
YET STRONG ENOUGH TO SHIELD ME FROM THE STORMS OF LIFE... HEALING
HANDS THAT COOLED THE FEVER OF A YOUNG ONE...PRAYING HANDS THAT
LED ME IN MY FIRST PRAYERS AT NIGHT...TEACHING HANDS THAT ROLLED
COOKIES AND PLAY DOUGH AND BAKED AND COOKED
THE MOST DELICIOUS CREATIONS!
I CANNOT DESCRIBE THE INDESCRIBABLE PLEASURE OF HOLDING
MY MOTHER'S HANDS IN MY OWN...AND FEELING DEEPLY INSIDE ME
THE LOVE AND THE CARE OF ALL THOSE YEARS.
HOW I LOVED THOSE GIVING, CARING, COMPASSIONATE AND
BEAUTIFUL HANDS OF HERS...THE MOST BEAUTIFUL HANDS
I HAVE EVER SEEN!
THESE MEMORIES FLOOD MY HEART!

Without A Sound

Without a sound she slipped away,
In the stillness of the night...
The time had come for her to leave,
In the glow of the pale moon light.
Without a sound she slipped away,
Into another world...
Carried gently by her Angel; wings unfurled.
Close by, we slept, just to be near
Our Mother Dear...
And while we slept...she left this world
With Jesus ever near.
Not one sound was made that night,
I believe she was at peace...
And silently, so silently,
She finally got release.
Sweet release from pain, from care...
From worries all around,
As she breathed her last breath on this earth,
She never made a sound.
Somewhere outside a bird still sings,
A feather floats from angel's wings...
This world goes on, but not the same,
One beautiful song does not remain...
Perhaps it does but we can't hear,
Her glorious rhapsody so near...
Her heavenly notes arise on high,
Caressing us as she passes by.

. . .

*(When I got home in the middle of the night, I found
a pink flower (which had come from my wreath on my house)
tucked tightly into my door stoop, where you had to step over it.
At first I thought it blew there...not a windy night...
No one else except family knew that Mom had died.
Also it had lightly snowed and there were no footprints,
anywhere...Mother loved the color pink....
The flower is still there...*

*If I go and prepare a place for you,
I will come again, and receive you unto Myself,
that where I am, there you may be also.*
John 14:3

PEACE IN THE VALLEY
APRIL 1, 2009

WE WERE IN BRANSON, MISSOURI.
I WOKE UP THINKING OF MOM.
WE HAD ALWAYS CALLED EACH OTHER TO TELL
A JOKE ON APRIL FOOL'S DAY OR SHARE A LAUGH.
SHE SURE KNEW HOW TO CELEBRATE LIFE!
SO, I BREATHED A LITTLE PRAYER UPON WAKING,
IN THANKS FOR HER,
SUCH A GREAT BLESSING IN MY LIFE!
WE WERE STAYING AT A VERY NICE HOTEL
AND WE THEN WENT TO BREAKFAST.
THE RESTAURANT HAD ONLY A FEW PEOPLE IN IT.
I NOTICED AN OLDER COUPLE SITTING AT A TABLE.
THE WOMAN HAD WHITE HAIR,
CLIPPED UP IN A BUN, HIKING BOOTS ON
AND WAS HOLDING A BOOK.
THEY TALKED A BIT AND HE LEFT.
SHE WASN'T READING, JUST HAVING HER COFFEE.
I TOOK A TABLE A COUPLE OF TABLES AWAY,
BEHIND HERS BY A HUGE WINDOW
WHICH OVERLOOKED THE VALLEY OF THE
OZARK MOUNTAINS. (WE WERE ON THE 9TH FLOOR
OF THE GRAND PLAZA HOTEL.)
A CD WAS PLAYING...THE FIRST SONG WAS,
"I BELIEVE," (MOTHER PLAYED THAT
ON THE PIANO ALL THE TIME).
THE NEXT ONE WAS, "THERE WILL BE
PEACE IN THE VALLEY FOR ME SOME DAY,
THERE'LL BE NO SADNESS, NO SORROW,
NO TROUBLE, NO TROUBLE I SEE,

...

THERE WILL BE PEACE IN THE VALLEY FOR ME,
OH LORD, I PRAY!"
I BEGAN TO VERY QUIETLY SING WITH THE SONG...
WHILE OVERLOOKING THE VALLEY BELOW...
THE ONE THING I MISSED SO WAS HOW MOM
ALWAYS HARMONIZED WITH ME!
SUDDENLY, I HEARD THE WOMAN AT THAT TABLE
QUIETLY HARMONIZING WITH ME...
SHE SLIGHTLY TURNED HER HEAD TO MY SIDE...
AND SANG IN A SWEET, BEAUTIFUL VOICE...
IN HARMONY, JUST LIKE MOM USED TO!
MY BREATH CAUGHT IN MY THROAT...AS I SANG...
THEN, ONE BY ONE, TWO WAITRESSES QUIETLY
CHIMED IN. IT WAS AN AWESOME GIFT!
I HAD TO STOP AND FACE THE WINDOW
TOWARDS THE "VALLEY," AS TEARS FLOODED MY EYES.
HERE WAS A GREAT GIFT STRAIGHT FROM HEAVEN!
WHEN I TURNED BACK, THE MYSTERY WOMAN
WAS WALKING OUT THE DOOR
TO THE ELEVATOR...I NEVER SAW HER AGAIN.
PEACE IN THE VALLEY, INDEED!
APRIL FOOL'S DAY...
THANK YOU, LORD, FOR THE GIFT!!!

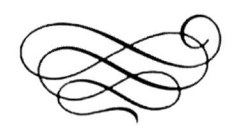

THERE IS A TIME FOR EVERY PURPOSE UNDER HEAVEN
A time to be born and a time to die.

The robins chipper in my ear
That Spring has finally dawned,
Determinedly, they build their nests
While trilling out their song.

The trees arrayed with leaves of green
Have finally come alive...
Through Winter's cold and harshest winds...
Somehow, they still survived!

The Iris and the Buttercups
And Lilacs all abloom...
Alive again, quite joyously
Break forth from Winter's tomb.

The signs of hope are all around
New life is now at hand...
Our Mom awakes in joyous song
In Heaven's promised Land!

Her Springtime dawns with radiant light,
Her beauty, unsurpassed...
Her joy and fullness evermore
In the Kingdom that will last!

There, beauty overwhelms the Soul,
In praise of God, most high...
And His sweetness fills the atmosphere,
As the Angels whisper by.

There are no more cares, no worries
No stress and no more pain...
Only gentleness and peacefulness
And happiness remain!

. . .

A sweet Norwegian Angel
Now makes the others smile,
And kisses all the children's cheeks
While humming all the while.

This Angel's name is Helene…
For, you see, she didn't leave
Us, all alone, down here, on Earth
To simply sit and grieve.

Be quiet now…Be still…Just Listen
With your heart, for you will hear…
A piano softly playing
By the one who plays "by ear."

Now just let her music fill you up
With peacefulness and prayer…
It's our Norwegian Angel;
She's just playing "Over There."

Her cheer is in the air you breathe
Her melody lingers on…
Her warmth and hugs caress us,
In the Cardinals' morning song.

She speaks to us in Sunsets
And consoles us through each other
You can feel the "Angel kisses,"
That could only be from Mother!

So, hush, be still and listen
For her softness still abides…
For she now lives on…Forever
And is always by our sides!

She's not as far as you may think
The veil is "oh, so thin"
So open up your heart…
And let her "Sun-Shine-In."

There is a time for every purpose under heaven. A time to be born and a time to die.
Ecclesiastes 3:1,2

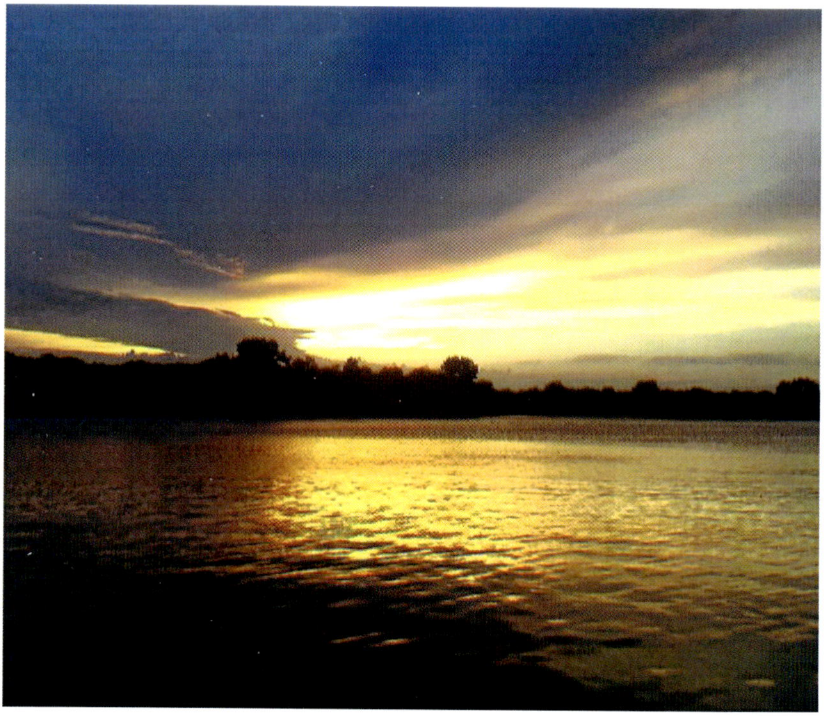

CHAPTER NINE
Reflections of a Cancer Survivor

Dear Reader,

I open my life and I share my experiences
with those of you who may need support and
encouragement during and after a cancer diagnosis;
in hopes that you might be encouraged
and renewed or uplifted.
I have survived cancer twice, aided with much prayer,
surgeries, radiation and chemotherapy.
I pray that you too, will find that throughout
your ordeal, you will be blessed and be strengthened
by God, through those who love, care and pray
for you. Angels will appear in the form of
loving people to strengthen you on your journey.
I send out my own prayer for you,
that you will find strength and love for your own
life situation which you are enduring.
May you be blessed to "Be Strong and
Carry On with your own Life's Song."

Reflections of a Cancer Survivor

It is summer, 2006, I'm just glad to be alive
The cancer, once again, I have survived.
The pain, the chemo, the surgeries,
What is God's plan in such as these?
A plan that keeps me on my knees!
Is it over? Am I cured? Will it return?
I'm not assured!
But for now, I will believe with all my heart
That by God's strength, I have been cured...
No more treatments, chemo no, only tests
To confirm it's so.
My "upside-down" world these 11 months long
Has been for me, a painful song.
A reality, beyond belief
Days and nights consumed with grief
Prayers and calls and cards from Friends
And Family, that an angel sends
To lift my spirits and help me know
That God is always in control.

. . .

And, so I praise Him, through my pain,
The trust and faith, my soul has gained;
Could not be won through sky's of blue
And endless days of bliss, that's true
His plan for me, my Lord knows best...
I must believe Him through this test.
The test of living...day by day...
Trusting that God will show the way!
This path, that leads me straight to Him...
And in my "yes" my soul shall win!

Trust in the Lord with all of your heart,
and lean not to thine understanding.
In all of your ways acknowledge Him,
and He will direct your path.
Proverbs 3:5-6

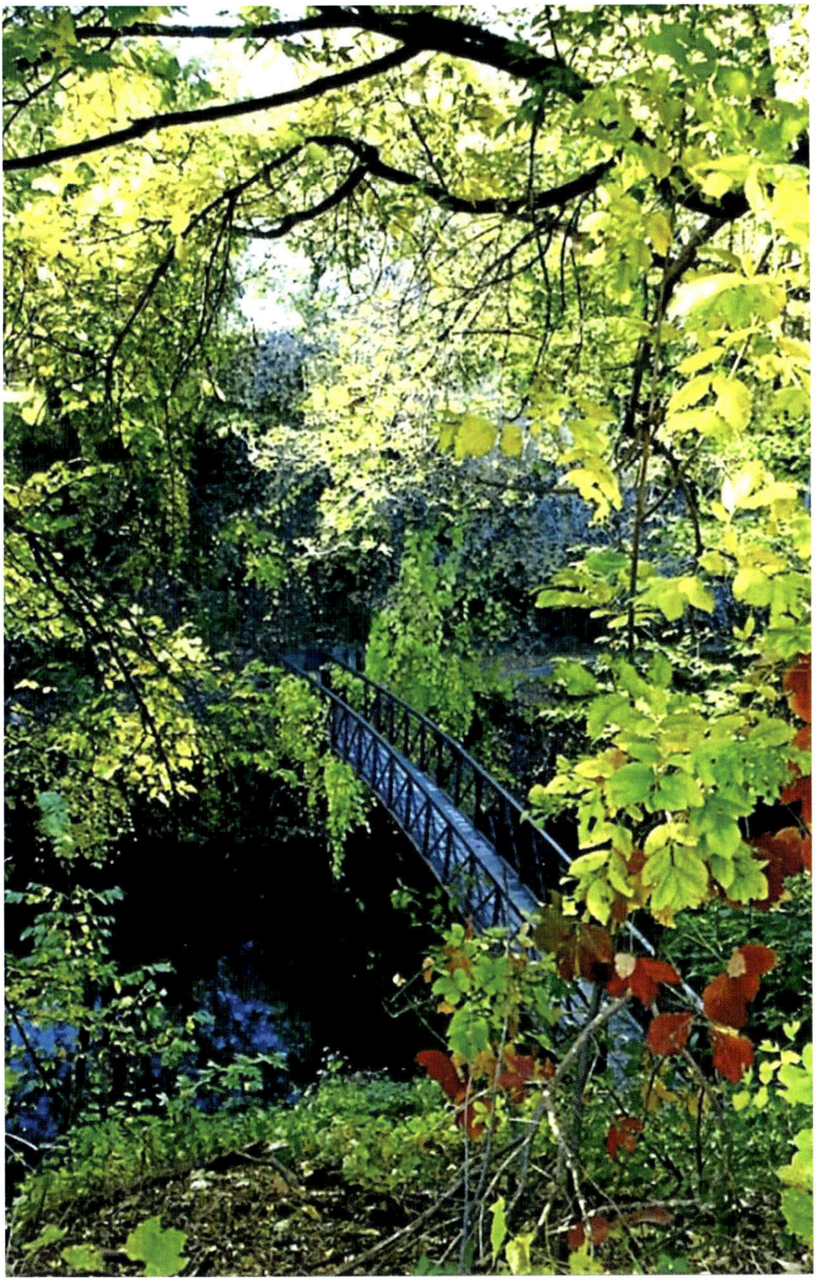

As One

When skies were dark, your light was there...
When pain was great, you showed you care.

When I was weak and frail and down,
And storm clouds threatened all around...
No longer could I stand alone...
Your prayers became my very own!
And lifted me out of despair,
And held my hand so I could dare
Go on.

Our steps became one step...
Our prayer became one prayer...
our hope...one hope,
our God, one God,
Surely, our hearts beat as one!

Dedicated to my dear family who lifted me high, in prayer,
during my cancer and treatment.

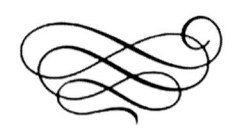

THE DANCE

Today I saw an eagle soaring high above the bay...
Soaring high and gliding, as if it were at play.
It wasted not a wing-beat
But rose and fell and glided...
Upon an un-seen wind it moved
As if it's fate were guided.

It seemed to be delighted
In its effortless advance;
It was then that I remembered, Gayle,
What you said about "The Dance."

Pain embraced for "love's" sake
Then, the spreading of one's wings
To catch the "flow of grace" that comes
To those, in need, who, to Him cling!

And those who see the eagle rise
Take courage and comfort from its flight
For there-in they shall see their God...
His power, His love, His might.

Written by: Dianne Goetten Krause

Set Free

My prison walls have been released
Relentless pain, which now has ceased.
Chemo-white skin I dreaded to see
Has gone...the color is back in me!
The spark I had, I've now regained
Only hidden scars, I have retained.
Overnight, my hair turned white
And now, is almost gone,
But in my mirror my hair is not
What I concentrate upon!
I see the sparkle in my eyes;
My voice is quick and strong,
The laughter now, I often hear
Sounds joyful, like a song.
The dread, which weighted my heart down
The death, that felt so near...
Is lifted now, I feel the joy
Instead of constant fear!
My future is uncertain, yes
Of that fact, I am most sure!
But for today, this moment, now,
I will believe my cure.

. . .

I joyfully sing out my praise
To God, who brought me through...
This awful hell and let me live!
His hand has made me new.
Out of death's grip, He brought me, twice!
A miracle to behold;
His kindness and compassion,
I proclaim, it must be told.
I sing...I dance...I praise His Name,
My life will always be...
Forever His, my precious Lord,
Again has set me free!

Sweet Assurance

He touched me; In despair and fear...
I felt my Savior very near; He touched me!
His loving arms were open, wide;
I felt His peace...down, deep inside.
I felt the strength infuse my bones...
No longer was I all alone!
HE touched me!
I know it now, I knew it then...
No matter what, no matter when;
If we just ask, reach out our hands,
His love will blanket all our plans!
No cross too heavy for us to bear...
Our lives, forever, in His care,
He touched me!

"My blessing prior to cancer surgery"

My prayer

My precious Lord and my God,
May I never, for one moment...
Forget your lavish kindnesses!
May I never, for one moment,
Forget that you hear every thought,
Every prayer whispered and un-whispered...
Even in the depths of my heart!
May I remember, and be glad...
Even in the pain and darkness of the trials
That shall surely come! May I ever rejoice...
For You, my God, are with me!
That, alone, is sufficient reason to sing!
For, I shall never be without you!
Remind me, Lord, for in my weakness, I fail!
Strengthen me, Lord, for in my pain, I falter!
Forgive me, my Lord, for my eyesight is dim in the darkness!
Lift me above myself, Lord, that I may always and
Forever praise you, my Creator, my Friend, my God!
This I ask, in the name of Jesus, who is Lord forever...Amen.
With Love, your Daughter

Written after my second cancer diagnosis.

Press on

Nothing could have prepared me for
the loss of a breast, thru cancer.
The news of cancer, itself, is horrific,
but I was certainly unprepared for the horribleness of the loss.
One is consumed with the dealings of cancer...
but to look down at your own chest and see an
ugly scarred hole is devastating, indeed.
It ripped my breath from my throat, soundlessly, I gasped;
As a groan and sob came forth from somewhere
deep inside my being.
The cancer, that you never knew you had; is gone!
So is the breast...that you loved; gone forever.
And so, you attempt to adjust.
You are blessed. The cancer is gone.
But you realize you must grieve.
Grieve your loss.
The grief that I tried so, to overcome and to hide,
is like an ocean wave...
Building and building rolling upward
From the depths...
Unstoppable, surfacing only, occasionally,
with a loud sobbing roll...
And then you go on again.
But like the ocean, it is endless, always
Just below the surface...ready to devour you...
when it's seemingly calm on the surface.
Part of me was always struggling to "keep afloat,
keep alive, keep hanging on, and keep smiling."

• • •

At times, we struggle over differentiating
His will from our own will.
But, when all is surrendered to His love...
The peace comes...
Slowly...
Steadily...
Constantly and surely.
The acceptance grows. The assurance lingers.
Our world expands.
His sweetness calms our fears.
And so, my life story continues...
For His own reasons, "I" continue.
Therefore, even the pain is exhilarating to my spirit...
For God is at work in me.

As we must prepare for the battle BEFORE it begins,
to stand strong in His army, I now prepare, in my spirit...
This is my preparation time...

To march on...
To press on...
To walk on...
Thru this next chapter of my life
That He has given me...
TO GOD BE THE GLORY.

"If calamity comes...we will cry out to you in our distress...
and you will hear us and save us."
2 Chronicles 20:9

Willow Whisperings

I am crunching along my yard in the colored leaves that have fallen.
I reflect upon the past year as I sit beneath my willow tree by the water. Up,
up, up, I peer into this bare willow.
I can see now that nearly half of one side of the tree is gone.
The storm hit it hard. And yet, I think to myself,
when the leaves are in full bloom, the missing side of my willow
is un-noticeable. My tree is so beautiful.
Birds still nest in its encircling branches and it still holds
my hammock so I can gently rock in the warm breeze.
It shelters and shades me.
My wooden swing solidly hangs from a branch
and supports me as I gaily swing towards the blue sky,
such deep green against a bright blue heaven and
the bark is rugged and twisted from years of wear.
So it is, with my own body, I think. One would almost not know
that beneath my clothing, I, too, have a missing side.
Perhaps, I too, am still beautiful in the sense of caring,
sheltering, helping, holding,
and maybe I'm stronger than ever before.
Maybe I can understand suffering more now.
Maybe I can re-assure others of hope...
for I have survived and seen hope come alive.
My willow is no less a willow...I am no less me,
But rather more of what God has called me to be.
For, the years have weathered me, and the storm has come,
I have been blown in the winds of change and
for God's own reasons, I have survived.
I am more rugged, perhaps, but stronger.
My willow is not a weeping willow!

• • •

It does not bend and hang it's head low to the ground
but rather lifts its arms to the heavens and praises its creator...
I shall do the same!
I lift my arms, my soul, to my Creator, God, and thank Him
for His wisdom, His strength, and for my willow whisperings.
I have seen winter's blast and darkened sky but
I know that Spring comes and life begins again!
TO GOD BE THE GLORY!

Written after my breast cancer and mastectomy, prior to my re-construction surgery.

In Japan, broken objects are often repaired with gold. The flaw is seen as a unique piece of the object's history, which adds to its beauty. Consider this when you feel broken.
Author unknown

The Master of Design

When the Master of Design builds a vessel,
He knows there will be storms and tempests and waves
that crash and depths of immeasurable proportions...
And, so the master builds this vessel with measures
to weather the storms and tides.
We will be tossed about.
We will fall, we will doubt.
But, we will prevail.
Life, itself, is an ocean.
At times, tranquil, peaceful, serene...
At other times, wind-swept storms,
tidal waves and hurricanes come sweeping around us,
washing over us, threatening to drown us!
He gave us promises suitable for these times
of distress and storms...
Promises we can lean upon and trust in...
to wear around ourselves and our vessel,
as a tried and true life vest, unsinkable!
Yes, we shall bob in the ocean's tempest, but we will not
go under to our death but rather stay afloat...
to the life, which He has promised
(Eternally).

...

*Let the sea rage around us, as we hold fast,
onto the Word,
The unsinkable Word of our Savior!*

But we have this treasure in earthen vessels, that
the excellency of the power
may be of God and not of us.
2 Corinthians:4-7

Waiting...Questionable Cancer Scan

This waiting thing, for tests to come back,
This limbo is like a hungry tiger
circling ever closer and closer around you.
Waiting to devour you... if you allow it to.
The fear of more cancer is the hungry tiger; the fear of the unknown.
The sheer terror, not of the physical tests,
Not of pain, but rather a maddening threat to devour your sanity...
if you give in to it.
Your faith reminds you of your protector, ever near, ever vigilant,
ever loving, ever caring, through any trial,
any danger any difficulty. You hang on. You hold it closer.
You know, through experience, that Aslan,
the lion (Christ) is more powerful than pain, than fear itself.
In that knowing, comes your strength to go on
to fight the tiger and not crumble.
And so, you step outside the circle, ever closer to this hungry tiger circling
around you. You stare into his cold eyes with your
eyes of trust and faith in the mighty and powerful one.

• • •

You step closer, and the tiger cowers,
slinking further away from you...but never leaves.
You claim the promise.
You walk on, in faith. Because the great Lion, Aslan,
would not have promised or lied to you when he said
he would walk beside you forever unto the end.
With Aslan, we step into our future, unknowingly,
yet trusting and are safe from the claws of the tiger.
Rest now, upon the tender and soft mane of Aslan and sleep...
let the tiger hide in the shadows for Aslan is awake.
For all is well. For whether we live
Or whether we die we are with the Lord...
All is well... "It is well; it is well, with my soul..."

Picture This

A good laugh after surgery:
I look out of my kitchen window.
Slippin' and Slidin' up the walk…here comes the two Lil'
Book-end sisters, marching along, heavily laden with food, gifts,
bags, flowers, in this, the dead of winter!
One's yackin' at the other one…lips a flappin'.
Laughter cuts thru the cold air…
I can hear them thru the closed window!
Once again, a journey to the North land
to cheer a sister, to take her hand,
to make her laugh, to lighten the load.
My Family has all made this journey,
my Husband, my Beautiful Daughters, my Sisters,
Mother, Grandchildren, Brother, & In-laws,
thru the years for reasons of love, to cheer,
to laugh, to listen, and to pray.
They somehow make even life's "sucky" moments
bearable and even fun.
This is my family…stronger, by far, than Superman
or Wonder Woman…bringing the healing touches
of the Great Physician, to one who is in need of care
and kindness and understanding.
And, I am exceedingly blessed, beyond belief!
I forever thank All of You! xo

*Bear one another's burdens,
and so fulfill the law of Christ.*
Galatians 6:2

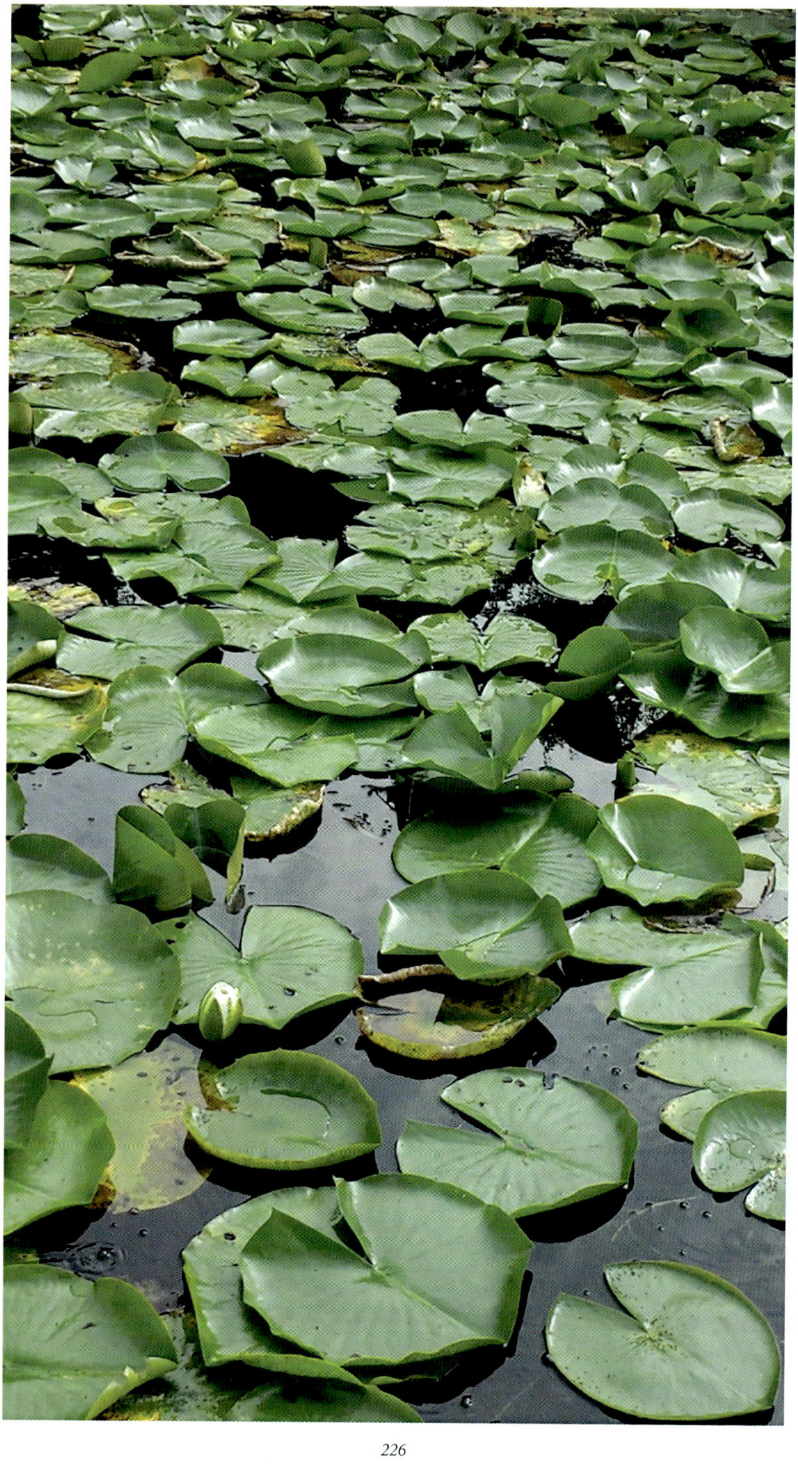

Heartfelt Tributes

Each of us has special moments
that stand out in our lives.
These moments are often committed to memory
and are not forgotten.
Gayle has captured these memories
and has shared them with all of us
through prose and poetry.
She has conveyed the song of her innermost heart
about what she has experienced
in relation to the unique events of her life.
As you read, you may come to cherish
the events of your own life more deeply
because of the music that she creates.
Your life, too, will sing a new song
after reading these wonderful thoughts.

A loving comment from "the spouse in the house"

To my beautiful, gracious, loving and generous Mother...
Your amazing talent for writing has touched us all...
With love and understanding for our fellow man...
And is EXTRAORDINARY beyond words!
You are a true blessing to all
who have the honor of meeting you!
Thank you for teaching me to "always be kind" to others
And for being the BEST MOM in the universe!
I love you to the moon and back!
XO

Lisa Marie

This is the story of a woman

who was given the gift of writing...

And so she wrote,

And wrote,

And she wrote some more...

Until one day she made up her mind that it was time...

Time to share her gift...

And the world was never the same!

This was a very personal journey...

One that included cherished moments...

A gift of time, really...

There was much love, laughter,

Tears and great JOY!

Her personal journey included...

miles and miles,

years and years,

of tender moments...

Special times,

Difficult times,

Challenging times,

Yet, all the time,

Trusting her Savior because He was always with her...

• • •

All of these moments caused her to become a woman who is...

Clothed with strength and dignity,

A woman who laughs without fear of the future,

Because...

She has learned,

To trust,

To love,

To give,

To be,

To Celebrate...

Through the laughter,

And, even through the pain...

And it is a very beautiful thing...

Precious.

This beautiful woman is...

My Mother.

I love you, Mom,

And I'm so proud of you.

-Bridget

xo

My Grandma has always told me
her poems and stories
which made me the person
I am today.
Love,
Sophie

♪♫

My Grandma has always found beauty in everything
and happiness in the dark times
and she has been such a role model for me.
Her poems really capture
the best moments in life.
Love,
Jack H. Nguyen

For all my life my Gramma has had a passion for writing,
but in a way that is often unseen.
Since I was young she has written
not for acknowledgement or fame,
but to show God's love, to encourage others in dark times,
and to keep memories alive that would have otherwise waned
into the forgetfulness of the past.
Her stories have served as a reminder of how sweet life is
by bringing me back to the vibrancy of life
experienced through a young boy's eyes
and the marvelous escapades I bravely overcame
while visiting Gramma & Grampa's house.
Her poems have been a source of inspiration
and Godly wisdom from a discerning and talented Woman.
She has a profound gift, and it is exciting to share in her adventure
of spreading her works for others to enjoy.
Love,
Alex Klinefelter

My Grandmother's book...
My Grandmother has been known by many for her
God gifted ability to bless friends and family
with her poems, short stories and heartwarming cards
that not only put a growing smile on your face
but will also touch your heart; showing her unconditional love
for others and her passion to write!
Love,
Matthew Klinefelter

"Black-capped Chickadee"
Original oil painting by Dianne Goetten Krause

Heartfelt Thanks
FOR ALL PHOTOS AND ARTWORK!

Cover Design: Gayle Goetten Piche'
Bridget Lea Halloran
Graphic Design: Terri Peterson
Jacket Photo Credit: Dianne Goetten Krause

Original Artwork:

Dianne Goetten Krause: Copies of her Original Oil Paintings; Wren & Lilacs, Violin & Flowers, Mountains, Mother's Bible, Lilacs, Angel, Cardinal, Birthday Cake, Black-capped Chickadee

Jack Henry Nguyen: Flower Design & Blue Rose

Photo Credits:

Bridget Lea Halloran: Potter and clay, sunshine and leaves, water lilies and goldfish, petals in air, crocus, willow tree, vine, leaves and bridge, rain drops.

Alexander Paul Klinefelter: Cherry branches, covered snow branches, snowflakes in air, ice, clouds, colored leaves.

Mary Elise Meichels: Butterfly on branch, old fashioned Christmas tree, butterfly on finger.

Dianne Goetten Krause: Water lilies, yellow flowers, white squirrel, pink peony, orange oriole.

Gayle Goetten Piche': shadows, hand and bird, woods and path, geese on lake, sunsets, clouds, sailboat, rainbow, moonbeam sliver, pussy willow, robin, ocean, willow tree, children with balloons, clouds and flag, lake & fireworks, angel kisses, snow baby, lantern, girls, blurry lights, tree and presents, elf on log, children, superman shoe, angels, Mom's hands, birthday cake, hands on piano, iron angel, waves, mist, sunset. Moon over lake: unknown.

Original Poetry Contributions:

Bridget Lea Halloran, Dianne Goetten Krause,
Kandace Goman, Helene Bergh Goetten

***All Scripture quoted has been taken from various translations.

*Things which the eye has not seen and the ear has not heard
and which have not entered the heart of man,
all that God has prepared for those who love Him.*
1 Corinthians:2-9